DELIRIUM

DELIRIUM

A NOVEL BY

Oliver Simmons

WEIDENFELD AND NICOLSON
London

ISBN 0 297 79576 7

Photoset, printed and bound in Great Britain by
Redwood Burn Limited, Trowbridge, Wiltshire

To my mother and my brother.
And to Rowan.

1

I'd been on the floor in the pub, literally. Eight pints of snakebite, each downed in one, one after the other, what an achievement! I was trying to amuse these two stony-faced girls who didn't want to talk to me.

'Eight pints, I mean, I know that some people would say that's a pretty crass and shallow achievement, and I agree with them if they do. But nevertheless,' I smiled and dropped to my knees with my chin and hands just above the table, 'it ranks as one of my all-time achievements, in fact today is a landmark in my whole shit life.'

Then this rockabilly girl I'd got a date with turned up. I'd completely forgotten about her. I told her about the British class system, the nature of humour, medal collecting. I insisted on trying on her jacket, but black bombers don't suit me. She left early, she left me in the pub, so I had a few more pints and went on to the Constipation Club.

In the Constipation I wandered around a bit, got in a few vodkas, talked to a few people, told a few jokes. I ended up with this Irish girl for the night. I was talking to her, about her hair or something, when she put a finger on my lips, pulled me to her, and gave me a long, exciting kiss. So I ended up in her bed somewhere in the suburbs of London; strange set-up there, loads of Irish girls all sleeping together, three to a bed, and some gay who kept grinning at me and at some point took his shirt off and stood smiling away.

I left in the morning, it's a good way to see London, you know, my lifestyle. On the train home I thought about the pub last night, and the club. I just couldn't remember much of it at all. Things weren't always like this, but now I just don't seem to care any more.

2

So a few years ago I did make the awful mistake of going up to university, to study English.

Now when people sell out, when they betray their friends, when they shit steal behind people's backs, and tell lies, they really have to go the whole hog, play the total bastard scumbag. It's very difficult to sell out only partially, once you stick your itchy toe in the swamp, you just have got to get sucked in, right up to your two-faced phoney smile.

Was I selling out, going to university? I was leaving crummy Camden Town and was starting a new wonder life in the Midlands. No more chips, no more smelly clothes, I was leaving it all behind. Was I selling out?

I was selling out getting a lift up there with my dad. Sneaking out of the house, sneaking into his expensive car. My dad left me and mum when I was about five. He ran off with some slag, he pissed off and left us. I don't want to get too heavily into all that, but suffice to say we all had a terrible time, got massively screwed up, and will probably never be able to feel happy or secure or safe now, ever.

So there was I, selling out, sitting next to him in the car, listening to his fascinating conversation.

'Yes, I'm pleased you're going up to university, get you out from home. Of course I wouldn't say it was exactly up to the place I went to, not exactly Oxford, but still, I suppose, it was the best you could do.'

I smiled, hands clutched, watching the road, wondering when would be a good time to ask if I could put on one of my tapes.

'You know, Jack,' Dad said, 'I could make life very easy for you if I wanted to.' He smiled thoughtfully. 'I could fix you up with a nice job, give you plenty of money, generally see you're all right.'

'Oh, that would be really great, Dad.'

'But you know,' he looked at me and gave a firm smile, 'I'm not going to help you, I'm not going to lift a finger to help you. You should go your own way.'

He smiled, I smiled.

'Er, Dad, could I put on this tape? It's quite jazzy, I think you'll like it.'

So we listened to my jazzy tapes, along with a bit of northern, as we drove up to my new university. And I thought of all those interesting intelligent people I'd meet, all the friends I'd make.

3

Now I'm standing in this pub snogging with this girl, it's just gone eleven, last orders have been taken.

'You know, you remind me of my primary school teacher, seriously, it's your eyes. She had big brown eyes just like you. I really liked her a real lot, you really do look like her.' I was smiling into her face, leaning over her, almost touching her. I put my hand on her shoulder, to steady myself.

'I could make you a star if I wanted to, you know, the big time, seriously.' I waved a hand around the room, 'Honestly I could if I wanted to.'

She did look like my old primary school teacher, as she gazed up at me with her nervous little smile.

I leaned forward for another bout of snogging. This one lasted about a minute and as we pulled away I made another lunge. She backed away now, and those big brown eyes looked hurt, almost afraid. But I hugged her back and forced it, looking in those eyes, they really were nice actually.

I left her for a minute and went over to my friend, Mark. He had one of those sickly smiles on his face, he was actually shifting his feet.

'Do you have to do that in the middle of the pub, I mean it's a bit fucking much, isn't it? I mean I don't exactly want to spend my time standing watching you snog with that poor girl.'

We looked over. She was waiting hopefully, she was – honest.

'Anyway, come on,' he said, 'let's hit the Slag Club now or we're going to have to queue for ages.'

He was right, about the queue for the Slag, and I wanted to go anyway.

'Oh, please don't go there,' she said, looking at me adoringly. 'Come to the Gutrot with me. My friend's got tickets, get you in free.'

Now this was nice, really nice. I mean she really was pleading, she was adoring. She was a bit too fat, though.

'Look, I'm really sorry.' And I was, fairly. 'If it was me I'd go with you but my mate here's really set on going to the Slag, and I did promise him I'd go as well.'

So I gave her my number and she swore she'd call me.

We hit the Slag. There are two ways of doing that, by the way, and I've done both of them.

Inside I bought Mark a drink, or to be exact, I bought my round, which by then was about number eight.

The first time I ever went to the Slag, Mark took me there. In those days it was a big step, a major breakthrough, you too could be a chosen one, a shining star, enter and leave your feelings of social inferiority behind in the fifth form.

Now the host of the club then was called Bjorn Toorun. Bjorn Toorun had been in a group who got into the charts. We used to read about him in music papers. Imagine the scene, my first visit to the Slag, Bjorn stands at the bar. He is a face.

'Bjorn Toorun,' Mark said. 'You know your song "Pacing the Park", well it's about me isn't it, you must have seen me on my regular walks, reading poetry, reciting

12

verse, compiling soul charts for my DJ's list. Let me buy you a drink.'

Mark held him in conversation for well over an hour, when they stopped talking, Bjorn shook his hand, gave him an invite to his next party.

'Proud to meet you friend, proud, real proud,' and he went off.

'Mark,' I said, 'that was brilliant, really brilliant, talk about respect from the stars. I mean that was Bjorn Toorun, I mean he was well impressed.'

Standing in the Slag now, a few years on, I look at Mark now, think how cool that was, what a brilliant thing to do.

'You were a fucking jerk tonight,' Mark said, 'snogging with that girl like a filthy lecher. Getting in your snog worth before closing time. And she must have been pretty disgusted as well, you saw the way she pulled away from you. You're turning into a filthy old lecher.'

Mark got the next round in. I had to sit down by then because my legs had given up on me. We both try hard to avoid the filthy stare of Bjorn Toorun, he thinks we're out to get him, he hates us, the stupid paranoid wanker. Why does everyone finish up like that?

4

'Look, why don't you just piss off,' Mark said to me. He was sitting in my living room. Some Spanish girl who I'd picked up that night had just left. She had said to me how much I fancied myself, what with my clothes and hair. I walked her to the bus stop and waited with her, to make sure she was safe.

'You are ideel,' she said.

'Oh thanks, that is a very lovely thing to say, I am very pleased you think so.'

'Ideel,' she said, 'I.D.L.E. You have nothing to do, so you wait for the bus with me. You are ideel, lazy, yes?'

Back in the living room, Mark said: 'Just piss off. I'm tired of hearing your boring voice, your boring self-righteous talk. You fancy yourself massively, you're so vain, you're so boring. Just piss off with your boring self-righteous shit.'

There was silence, I had expected this, or something like it, all day. 'You know, this sort of atmosphere, what you're saying to me, reminds me of – '

'I don't want to hear your fatuous shit, your crass analogies. Fuck off,' Mark said.

So we sat for about twenty minutes in silence and eventually Mark went. I sat alone, smoking in the living room.

Now I don't agree with Mark, I think he is fundamentally wrong. I really do, I'm sure. What he said, its whole content, tone, the whole lot, reminded me exactly of what Lucien had said to me a couple of months earlier.

'You're a wanker,' Lucien shouted. We were in the pub, everyone was listening.

'I mean you used to be all right, but now you're just a wanker. Why don't you just piss off now, fuck off. You make me sick. I mean, I'm telling you this because I'm your friend, I'm a real friend. You're a wanker. This pub makes me sick; full of poseurs, all looking at each other to see what they're wearing. Your attitude makes me sick. You must understand I'm your friend, I really am. You're a wanker. Fuck off, just fuck off.'

Now I think that Lucien is a jealous scumbag. I think he's talking shit because he's ugly, can't pull the women, he desperately wants to be trendy, he's just massively jealous. To round it all up, as Lucien would say himself, he's a wanker.

Having said all that, do they have a point? If they do it's a minor one, I know that. Is it all shit? I need more drink, badly, much more, pints and pints.

5

When you're like I am, when you decide to soak your brain in alcohol, you develop some sort of affinity with people like Bjorn Toorun. Fellow drinkers, fellow clubbers. Alcohol makes me generous, free-spirited, vulnerability becomes deeply endearing. Alcohol gives me an insight into man's frailty.

In this drink-sodden world, women seem to take on a strange, unfathomable, hostile mode. I suppose it's fair enough, they won't tolerate piss-heads talking to them, but even so. Yes, really, this attitude of theirs doesn't do them any good in my eyes. It gives me the impression that they despise weakness, it makes them seem hard and cruel. And when I talk to them, I know that if I'm going to get on with them I have to impress them, I have to talk about money and success, I have to make them look up to me, respect me. But that's absurd, because it's all a lie, because I really want to tell them about the huge despair I feel, that my life is one long, endless, dark night.

So, old, childish, laughable male values become endearing. Football cards, collecting things, clubbing it in a sixties style – all that sort of thing.

So here's a sad, shattered male dream for you, Bjorn Toorun's dream. For all its blind worship of a nonsense-cred world, for its foolishness, its frailty.

Bjorn Toorun lies twitching in bed, his eyelids flick, his limbs stir restlessly. Beside him, his tall blonde girlfriend sits up, smoking, watching him. Bjorn is having a dream, the same sort of dream shared by many of the Slag's regulars. The sort of dream that the Slag once existed for. An old-fashioned dream now, that recurs to Bjorn often in his sleep.

In it Bjorn is sitting in a Parisian bar, huge wooden fans cool the air above his head. He stirs his long drink and watches the pale shutters on the tall windows shift softly in the breeze.

'Sitting around me are my friends,' Bjorn mouths in his sleep. 'All my friends, the place is full. Next to me is J. D. Salinger, smoking a cheroot.'

'Hey, Bjorn, come here boy, right up close now. I must confide in you.' So I lean over towards his smiling features. He gives me a long appraising stare, his eyes widen in surprise, and he blows a great lungful of smoke in my face.

'Na, hey, only kidding, Bjorn, just messing, listen,' he tousles my hair, he pats my hair like a father to his own son. 'You're a terrific guy, Bjorn. Man, you are *not* a phoney, I mean that. You know,' he raises his voice now so that the whole place can hear, 'You and Holden, you got a lot in common, you really remind me of the little guy, you hear that, people? Now isn't he some kinda terrific?'

Sitting on my right is Colin McInnes. He is wearing black shades, a broad-brimmed Homburg and a huge baggy black-and-yellow check suit. For a while he does some fast jive talking with Courtenay, a young black musician. Colin turns to me: 'Ah, Bjorn, my good fellow, how are you? Remember last week when you and I re-worked the ending of *Absolute Beginners* while punting down the Seine? You got so carried away you actually fell in the river and an old lady dived in and pulled you to safety by your hair.'

I laughed at the memory, Colin's a good friend of mine.

For a while I wander round the bar, catching pieces of conversation from the assorted groups that have gathered, the musicians, artists, poets, writers.

'Bjorn, could I have a word?' Hick Doochok stands at my side nervously, I'm significantly taller than Hick. 'You remember that time when we disagreed on Kafka's philosophy, when we argued over whether to play the flip side of a record or not, when I said that you'd never be a success. Well, Bjorn, I want you to know that I was wrong and you were right on all counts. I'm sorry, Bjorn, forgive me.'

I smile and forgive. Hick looks unsteady, drunk, he sways and topples over. On his knees he is disgustingly sick in front of everyone. He actually crawls out of the joint. Poor Hick, embarrassing for the guy.

I stroll over to the bar and stand tapping my feet to the mellow latin jazz. The band finish the number and I catch Johnny the trumpeter's eye. 'This one's for you baby,' he says, as they launch into a snappy little number.

'Yo, Bjorn, Yo, Yo.' I turn round, the whole bar's shouting my name. 'Yo Bjorn man,' they all shout. 'We're your friends, Bjorn, we like you, we really really *like* you.'

But wait a minute, who are those two guys over there, talking to Colin and Mr Salinger? It's not, it can't be them, the two blokes from the Slag. It is – it's them. What are they saying? Colin looks at me, he's frowning. Salinger's shaking his head. *What* are they saying?

The room begins to sway, I'm spinning round the room, faces stare up at me disapprovingly. And now I'm running, I'm being chased by those two blokes. Where am I? Where am I running? It all looks horribly familiar. I'm running through Soho, it's the opening film sequence from *Absolute Beginners*. Jesus, now this really *is* becoming a nightmare!

But my path's blocked, a huge mound of filofaxes covers

18

the road. I start to climb them but half-way up the pile I start sinking. I clutch for air as the diaries begin to pull me down, to suck me in. The names and addresses of a thousand faces are crushing me, I'm suffocating.

Bjorn Toorun screams and wakes up covered in sweat. 'Shit,' he says, 'the same fucking dream every night.'

6

Now what was I doing with my head stuffed down a toilet? Oh yeah, I remember, I was puking up. It was on holiday in Greece, just recently. (It was quite pleasant actually, puking, really quite a nice, easy feeling.) Now I'd started on beer, just a couple, then we went on to the Flamingo Bar. Now that place really was hysterical, it really was just full of permed, oiled slimebags. But the best thing was the cocktails. They were the bar staff's revenge. I've seen it all before, believe me, Majorca, Minorca, been there mate, done it, seen it. I've seen the bar staff's revenge countless times, and it's always the same. Most times I'm the victim. I don't mind a bit.

What they do is get you on cheap drinks first, special offers. They always know the ones to pick, they always pick me, they always pick any English male. Anyway, they start you on cheap ones, little cocktails, or maybe cheap beer. After about the fourth or fifth, they've got you. Then the real bastard cocktails start appearing, and after three of those you're gone, and it's then they steal your women.

You see they know you're a failure, that you're not going to get those birds, 'cos those birds have come for a bit of foreign. So they immobilize you, just so as you don't get ratty when they steal your women. Simple but effective.

Anyway, as one does when on holiday, I'd formed an alliance with an English couple, and we were sitting by the pool after our trek around the bars. Now the evening had mostly consisted of Roger, Julie's husband, throwing a progressively deeper sulk as the drinks went down. It had started off all right with him buying the first round.

'So what do you think of the place then?' I asked cheerily. 'Nice beach but don't think much of the hotel food, eh?'

'Yeah,' he laughed. 'Terrible food it is, but those beaches, I tell you, beautiful, mate, absolutely beautiful. Good to meet other English people here, you know. Don't think much of these bloody Greeks, the prices they charge.'

'You're telling me, I'm sick of getting ripped off. Why, only the other day . . .'

So the first twenty minutes went OK. Safe ground, fellow nationals, bit of a hearty slag-off of the place, another beer. But then his wife started joining in.

I mean, God knows, I'm always massively tactful, you've got to be, unless you're a scumbag. But unfortunately, like most women out with their husbands/boyfriends, she was out for a bit of a flirt, something to keep her bloke on his toes, to make him wary, edgy. Something to make him knock back the drinks in double quick time, to make him hostile, to make him cry on her shoulder at night, to make him thoroughly miserable.

'Here, why don't you take your jacket off, you look ever so hot. You know, I'm sure I've seen your face before, didn't I say, love, that I'd seen his face somewhere? You're joking, you used to be a mod, hear that dear? That's how we met you know, when we was both mods.'

Wherever I go, to the far reaches of the world, I'm sure to bump into ex-mods. It's always the way. You can always be sure to meet them on holidays: on the beach, in the bar, at the airport. I can always tell them and they can always tell me. It's something about the way you wear your clothes, that sixties cut, you never really lose it. It's something about the . . . Sorry.

Have you ever tried pretending that someone is speaking to you when they're not? Have you ever stood nodding your head, agreeing, disagreeing in the most congenial way, with someone who is just blankly staring you in the face, saying absolutely nothing? I have. I was doing this there, to Roger, while his wife talked on to me. God, I really *tried*, I really did my best to make out his wife was not focusing all her attentions on me, but it was no good. As is the way of the male, Roger began to hate me. A deep begrudging hate that grew stronger as the drinks went down.

We sat by the pool, all three of us completely bloated by alcohol. By now Julie had attempted to push me in the pool, had forced me to take off my jacket, had insisted I had triple measures of the last duty-free rum. Roger sat in stony silence. I tried to tell a joke. Julie was in stitches, Roger looked pretty bloody low.

Oh, sod it, I thought, I was too pissed to really care, I mean I had tried so hard to cheer up the poor bastard, so I just joined Roger's silence and listened to Julie tell me what a really nice person she thought I was.

Firstly, it had been baking hot all day, secondly I had had a phenomenal amount to drink, thirdly Julie kept saying jump in the pool. I mean, it was still really hot, and the pool looked quite pleasant. Well, I must have been pissed.

'I'm going in the fucking pool,' I said. 'Never mind the sharks, fuck 'em. I'm going in.'

Then I took all my clothes off.

I stood there for a bit, swaying at the water's edge, it didn't look all that inviting. I turned round to bid Roger and Julie farewell, but there was Roger carrying his wife up the stairs, very unsteadily, back to the hotel.

''Bye darling, see you darling, ta ta darling,' called a smiling, cheerful Julie.

'Er 'bye, Julie, see you, Roger.'

Roger said nothing, he just carried on walking up those stairs and didn't look back.

So I went back to my room, stuffed my head down the toilet, and puked up. It was, seriously, the only thing to do.

7

I do love my dad, as much as you can love anyone who splits up your family, plays you off against your tearful mother. Who kicks you and your mother out of your home so that he and his wife can buy a better home for themselves with the money saved from paying the mortgage on your own home. Who is quite happy never to see you again. Who you have to book an appointment to see and when you turn up keeps you waiting for an hour, and then gives you twenty minutes of his time.

Now, basically, my dad really knows nothing about my life, he doesn't know my personality, he takes no interest whatsoever in what I do or say. To him I am just a financial burden. 'An annoying little bastard who only sees me when he wants money.' So when he does see me it's really quite embarrassing.

It was embarrassing sitting opposite him in the restaurant that day he took me up to university. He mentioned something about my looks.

'I think you should let your hair grow longer at the sides. I really do. You see your head is too narrow for that haircut.' We sat smiling at each other, our faces were beginning to ache. 'I hope you enjoy this place, it seems pleasant enough. You've got to remember that you're from London, though. That's very important. You've got to realize that you've had a very different background from most of the other people here who are probably from small provincial towns.'

We sat in the otherwise deserted restaurant, a surprised and embarrassed pair. It was like meeting your teacher out of school when you're with your mum. The 'niceness' was confused and forced. There was a sort of understanding, but it had to be concealed.

We went to my hall of residence to put my stuff in my new room. When he drove off I was really sad. I think in a way he knew what he was leaving me to. He drove off in his big car and I thought, fuck it, I don't want to talk to anyone.

8

I really did have some rather strange views about life when I first went up to university. For instance, I believed that women were a sacred breed who should be treated with respect and reverence. I thought that there were certain standards of behaviour to follow. That you had to 'court' a woman first. Also I thought that each individual had something to give in life, was his own unique creative being. I respected the morality of religion, the laws of philosophy, the great works of literature. I marvelled at the giants of literary criticism. I idolized the poetic form. I was a seriously deluded person.

In the deluge of campus life, in the fierce war of backstabbing and ego power, I did have one very powerful weapon. This weapon, which I never thought of as such until later, had what might be called a double-edged blade. What I'm talking about is my London upbringing – something all those provincials mistakenly envy.

Now I would be the last person to use this on anyone, in fact the whole thing's a load of rubbish and I have very little time for it at all. But on the other hand, when you're being despised for possessing it, when it's being used as a means to attack you, then you can really turn it on. I should stress here that I never, ever, started out using the London street bit, because I had, as I've said, all these ideas about the uniqueness of the human soul in its own creative potential, the beauty of naivety, the joy and importance of innocence.

That's where I fucked up badly, thinking that other people had a lot to offer. Thinking that despite the fact that someone is overtly provincial in outlook, says nothing of interest during a conversation, openly despises you for your unwanted charity in talking to them, that they've actually got something to offer behind the hostile, disinterested exterior. Believe me, they haven't.

I know it's an old cliché to categorize students in terms of workers, dossers, sporting types, trendies, Christians, etc., but let me tell you this, students as a whole are just one big boring cliché. It's almost as if someone in power is seriously taking the piss, handpicking the most ludicrous, obvious examples of each type of pond scum from society and shoving them in university to bond them together in little mutually hostile groups.

Ah! I said the word 'groups', that word – I kid you not – is going to make you shit it after I've been through with you. That word 'group' certainly makes me want to vomit excessively.

Anyway, the whole lot, all students, can be named under one category, and I must emphasize here that it applies to all strata of students. The category name is Retards. Each group likes to think of their other closest rivals as retarded in some respect. It's each group's reason for existence.

The first day on campus, wandering round the refectory, I sat down next to Tim and struck up a hearty conversation. Why did I choose Tim to talk to? Why indeed? Because Tim was the ugliest person I could see. He had appalling acne, his hair had been cut under a pudding basin, he smelt, his clothes were ten years old, his trousers barely reached

his ankles, he wore trainers. Great, I thought, a real no-
nonsense person.

'All right, mate, how goes it?' I asked heartily, hoping I'd
hit the right tone. I put down my coffee and six packets of
bacon crisps. 'So what do you think of this place. Not bad
eh?'

'Hello,' said Tim. 'L-l-l-l-like it here. It's v-v-very nice.'

'Yeah,' I said (must ignore the stutter and the haircut).
'So then,' I leaned back in my chair, 'what do you think of
the current political climate? Tepid, volatile?'

'I d-d-d-don't really know m-m-much about p-politics. I
m-mainly r-r-read science fiction b-b-books. Do y-y-you
read any?'

'Yes. I've read several, but I do find that genre rather
limited in its outlook. Er, what sort of music do you like?'

'M-m-mainly c-classical.'

'Oh, right, yeah. I like soul mainly. Seventies, northern
and sixties. I like the odd bit of jazz too. Bossa Nova,'
(which incidentally, was undergoing a revival at the time)
'and jazz blues singers, mainly Billy Holliday and Ella
Fitzgerald.'

So, having found a true soul-mate, I hung around with my
buddy, Tim, for a couple of days. But surprisingly, several
problems arose in our friendship. Firstly, Tim didn't go out
– he didn't go out at all. At five prompt he made it back to
his hall, queued up for his meal, went to his room and
studied astro-physics for five hours. This meant that I
trekked up to the union bar on my own, sat in a corner and
downed ten gin and tonics. Secondly, Tim didn't like me.
This was a major problem which I did my best to over-
come. But the more I was friendly to him the more Tim
grew to detest me.

'Y-y-you're really stuck up, aren't you?' he said once,
after I'd spent an hour telling him my views on politics and
the state of the world. 'Y-y-you reckon yourself, w-w-with

all your f-f-f-fancy clothes. You sh-sh-should realize th-th-that clothes d-d-d-don't matter, it's personality.'

I agreed. I couldn't have agreed more. I mean, why did the stupid bastard think I was talking to him in the first place. It was no good, Tim looked down on me. I just wasn't up to his standards. So after only two days he totally ignored me. The next time I saw him, he was with a group of people who all seemed to be massively taking the piss out of him. He had a big beaming smile on his acne-ridden face. He'd found friends.

9

Third day at university, something in my pigeon hole:

> The Dean of the Faculty of Arts has pleasure in
> inviting you to a reception for first-year students at
> Turd Hall. 8–10 p.m.

And what a joke that was. I mean, I went in there, with my
sad little clothes, all carefully thought out, and I came out of
there, spat out like a piece of shit.

I went into Turd Hall, delightful old Turd Hall, with my
head spinning with love and gifts and knowledge. I wanted
to meet friends, I wanted to meet clever people, I wanted to
drink all the wine in the whole place. No, that's not true,
strictly speaking: I didn't set out to drink all the wine, but
when, after just a few minutes I'd seen another human
wasteland, I just had to sink loads of the stuff.

Interestingly enough, the Dean, the dear old Dean, got
pissed as well. I never saw him again. I never saw anyone
there again, or I don't remember anyway. It was that kind
of innocence, it must have been pretty early on, when I still
had some dignity, because after a few days I remember
everyone I meet, so I still must have had some pride not to
remember any of those people.

I started talking to this boy with fair hair and glasses, a sloaney type. A public-school type. An English type. A sort of decent-chap type. And of course, wait for it, that fucker despised me. He hated me.

'All right, then, what do you think of the place? Plenty of wine eh?' I said to him.

'It's quite nice actually. Bit of a wine addict are you? Not bad stuff really. So what course are you on?'

'English.'

'Oh right,' he said. There was this sort of awkward smile on his face. 'Actually I'm doing English as well, seems like a pretty interesting course actually. Don't really fancy the old stuff though, but I'm so looking forward to getting really heavily into some of the lesser-known Shakespeare.'

'Right.' Great, I thought, Shakespeare is a terrific writer, I can really relate to this guy. 'I'm really interested in studying twentieth-century stuff myself, especially Lawrence. His ideas on women fascinate me.'

So presumably we talked a bit, while I was knocking back the wine, and, presumably, an intense dislike for me took shape in this bloke. I wondered about his past, his meaning in life. I looked at his brown cord jacket, his wire-rimmed glasses, green cord trousers, brown leather brogues. For some reason I pictured his mother calling out to him, 'Adam, come in now. Adam, come and meet these people. Adam, your father's on the phone. Adam, Selina's waiting for you.' I didn't really see a lot in this bloke, so I didn't really mind that he despised me.

But I did really. I was massively hurt, so I just kept knocking back that wine.

I suppose me and him must have cut quite a dash, amongst the five million girlies that surrounded us in their long skirts and frizzy hair. That's why, probably, this tutor came up to us and asked us if we wanted to be on this staff/student committee. But just as we rounded on him another tutor grabbed his arm.

31

'Come over here, Nigel, there are two girls over here who seem interested in the committee.'

So we lost that one, we lost that one to the girlies, just like we lost everything else that night – any literary sensibility, any male togetherness, we lost it all to the girlies. Such is the plight of the male student of English literature: you lose it all to the girlies.

Then the Dean called us all to order, stood in the middle of us, and tried to speak. Except he couldn't because the dear old bloke was so tight. It was while he was trying to speak that I started laughing. I really let it all go. I remember other people laughing too, girlies, that sloaney bloke, the Dean. After a bit I was the only one left laughing, just couldn't stop. I really couldn't. The Dean made his little speech of welcome over my laughing. He and the rest were smiling at me.

'I think we've all had a good old bit to drink. I wish you all well,' he said, grinning. He nearly fell over, he was really tight.

Funnily enough, that was the only civilized treatment I ever remember given to the students by the staff. It was a really nice atmosphere and everyone was smiling and drunk. And it was only my third day there. But when I left Turd Hall, I left alone. I crawled back to my room alone, no friends, no girls. All that effort, all that knowledge, totally unwanted. I mean, I suppose I was spat out like a piece of shit, but I can't help smiling about that evening, now that I think of it.

10

It's Societies Day at university – day number four of my stay. I traipse around the big hall looking at all the stalls. Most people by now are in groups or pairs, but I'm still on my own. Sad isn't it?

I signed up for CND, the Jazz Club, and the Labour Party. On the Jazz Club stall there's this tasty girl who gives me a broad grin. Someone remarks on my jacket, I struggle about, I'm embarrassed. You know it's still pretty exciting, everything's new and those girls, well, I mean.

I'm afraid this is pretty excruciating, but I went along to this Labour Party meeting and volunteered to be my hall rep. What was really bad was my conversation after the meeting with Joshua, a fellow rep.

Imagine a very nasal voice, a nasal twang. Picture NHS specs with a plaster holding together one corner, mad red curly hair, horrendous braces on his teeth. Think once again of the obligatory ankle-length trousers in tasteful brown nylon, the oldfashioned black training shoes. Remember Tim? Here was one of the same school, that same fine breed, but with political views!

I will say one thing for Tim. His hostility towards me

wasn't immediate, it just grew very rapidly the more I talked to him. In strictly cynical terms you might say that this indicates a certain naivety on his part as to judging whom he dislikes. Now with Joshua, the Labour rep, there is no delayed dislike, no naive interest in what's on offer. With Joshua we have immediate character judgements – old Joshy disliked me the *second* he saw me.

'It's nice to have a *trendy* lefty in among the ranks you know. I hope you realize that we take our politics very seriously,' Joshua sneered, his voice was incredibly nasal – the twang on the word 'realize' was something else!

'Oh yeah, of course, I mean I take it seriously. I'm a committed socialist. I really am.'

I looked down at my little yellow membership card. The constitution of the Labour Party, clause IV (4), it read underneath:

> To secure for the workers by hand or by brain the full fruits of their industry and the most equitable distribution thereof that may be possible upon the basis of the common ownership of the means of production, distribution and exchange, and the best obtainable system of popular administration and control of each industry or service.

Good stuff, I thought. I can dig that. But you know, Joshua, the old bastard, was right, because he and I did have different political views. Or rather we viewed politics in a different way. Joshua, was heavily into doctrine, the paper work, the manifesto, the cast iron rules and regulations of the party. Whereas I viewed politics with what I called a socialist perspective, whatever that means. Well what I meant by it was that I believed in the welfare state, altruism, the common good. I would always vote Labour but I couldn't get into all that party dogma. In fact he lived for the party, the Labour Party, the student Labour Party, the university branch of the student Labour Party, the twenty

34

strong members of the university branch of the student Labour Party, the three regular attendants of the twenty strong members of the university branch of the student Labour Party. This was Joshua's life, his bread and water.

Student politics were to Joshua all-consuming and all important. Interesting and important things like the colour of the society's meeting room, Joshua made into political issues.

And all this, all this character analysis and assassination, took place within just twenty minutes of talking to Joshua. So we parted company and ignored each other studiously ever after.

Now all this was pretty depressing. I'd just had too much hostility for one day. So that night, for a change, I went up to the union bar and downed about ten gin and tonics. Sitting there on my own, sighing occasionally, while the rest of the students merrily frolicked about.

11

Let me take you back to London, to present what fun things are happening in my life now.

'This conversation's bullshit, I'm gonna get another beer,' said the American, and walked off. And what a wanker he was!

'This conversation's bullshit.' Imagine that in a whiny, sneery brat voice, in a self-loving, bored, petulant American voice. What a twat! Mark came back. It was he who'd held the bloke in conversation for over an hour.

'Has he gone?' Mark asked. 'I hope he's not coming back. I tell you, that bloke, I was giving him my best "I've been to America" bit. The whole lot – politics, music, religion. So after about half an hour I started hustling for a pint. Perfectly fair. I'd given real conversation. I mean, American, big dollars, working as well, plenty moolah. The tight bastard wouldn't buy me one, so then I laid in a bit. No culture, purely materialist society, racist, unappreciative of the brilliant black music coming out at the moment. I hope he was offended. Was he offended?'

'Oh yeah, you wound him up really well. He pissed off fast. I mean, when you'd gone, having seen the way things were going and his sneery attitude, I started laying in a bit as well. I said the only thing America had done for us was music and fast food. He was well pissed off.'

So we drank some more, slightly unnerved and disgusted by the American, who was on his own and hustling for friends anyway.

Have I told you about this pub? It's my local, the Catcrap, and I'm down here most nights. Things are getting pretty bad because there're quite a few girls here tonight who I've had something to do with, plus their assorted friends and twat-heads galore.

First there's Lucille, who's just given me her number, and I've agreed to meet tomorrow. Now she's a wind-up, as Mark says, but I don't really care. She said 'fifty pence' so I gave her fifty pence and she got herself a coke. Last time she took one of my badges, the time before it was a full pack of cigarettes. But I don't care. I really don't, because I know I could sleep with her. I know I could. She fancies me, you see, so however much she takes liberties, I know I've got one over her. In this sick immoral world that we live in, once you screw a girl, once you snog with a girl, you've got a hold on her forever. This means you can smile at her when she's with her friends, you can brush her cheek when you're pissed, as you walk past to get another drink. You can say a hearty hello, with a meaningful look, when she's with her new boyfriend, and then watch him sweat. Actually, I don't want to live in a world where women are claimed like this. It makes me massively sad.

Secondly, while I've been talking to Lucille, this German girl I got off with two days ago at the Rat's Puke just walked past and gave me a filthy look. Having had a massive snogging session the night before, I got all matey with her the next day as we lay on the grass in Regent's Park. Sitting amongst the duck shit I decided to do my nice guy bit – inoffensive jokes, self-deprecating remarks, phoney

37

laughs, 'who, little old me?' To be strictly fair, she was boring the shit out of me, as practically all foreigners do. With her 'I like the Green Party, over here we smoke lots of grass, I like much of your underground music,' the usual bland stuff. You know, you can't help feeling a bit of national pride when you talk to foreigners, the old 'isn't Britain terrific, aren't we just so intellectually superior, isn't our music and fashion just streets ahead?'

As I once astutely pointed out to Mark, most of Europe is still stuck, I mean trendy Europe by the way, in hippy bullshit. Us Brits have moved on to sell-outs and cynicism and the Americans have moved on nowhere as their hippy movement was a load of shit anyway. But the dear old Europeans are still stuck in diddy dope land. I mean mainly the Netherlands and Germany, probably other surrounding countries too. So that's why you get all this Green Party shit, all this naff music, all this 'I like punks, some of them have got a lot to say.' Bullshit. Brits who do this sort of pose should be ashamed of themselves. I mean there's so much more on offer over here. But I'm getting ahead of myself. What am I talking about, 'there's so much more on offer'? Who cares? Most people certainly don't. Most people don't even know what's on offer.

Anyway, the thing with this German girl was that I'd seen her the day before in the pub and totally blanked her. A real obvious blank, just a day after my Mr Nice Guy bit. At the moment I'm seeing this girl Tulip. Luckily Tulip wasn't there tonight, but her friends were! Hairdressers one and all, Siegfried Baboon's finest cutters, a veritable mafia. I've got a horrible feeling that they might have seen me talking to Lucille, who luckily left the pub early, but even so.

The hairdressers sit in a circle around the steps of the Catcrap. Harry, who cut my hair yesterday, is talking to Sean, who's friends with Julia, who I went out with briefly about a month ago. Tulip is best friends with Harry and knows Sean and Julia. They all know John, who used to be

38

best friends with them all and now only talks to Sean. Felix, Rodney and Niki are all nearby. They used to work in the same salon as Sean and John before Rodney set up a place with Niki. This caused a bit of bad feeling with Sean and Tulip and Harry naturally sided with him against them. Niki's spending a lot of time gazing at Steven. She really badly wants to cut his hair, but we all reckon she's onto a loser.

I sit down in the middle of the group and try and start a conversation with Harry, the one who cut my hair yesterday. Now Harry's talking to Sean and doesn't really want to talk to me. In fact, Harry's positively sucking up to Sean in a big way. The nice thing about this situation, the really satisfying thing, is that Sean very obviously doesn't like Harry. He plainly thinks that Harry is a jerk. And the outcome? Sean directs all his attentions to me. Now I don't really care about Sean. I think he's a bit of a jerk himself, but since Harry's ignored me, I'm going to lap up Sean's attention.

So there's me and Sean talking like best buddies for a while, clasping hands, back-slapping, finger-clicking. And the funny thing about all this is we both know that neither of us really gives a toss about the other.

A few girls walk past who I've got off with. I eye up a few more who look like potential prospects. Mark joins me, we stand next to the circle of hairdressers. It's drinking-up time. The last few tramps and gippo children make their way past the pub to their doss for the night, shouting and stealing as they go.

I say goodbye to the hairdressers. Harry, deprived of attention and status, chooses to become all pally with me. He leaps on my back and does his frequent 'ho, ho, I'm gay' bit. I laugh with him to make him feel better. You see I never could piss on people. It's one of my great failings.

Mark and I walk off, past the canal, past the gippo camp. I hear a rustling in the rubbish outside the camp.

'Watch this,' I say. 'Let's see what this will produce.' And I throw a few chips on the pile. The rustling gets louder and a great fat grey rat appears, hurdles the heap, steals a chip and scuttles away.

We walk by the canal, down the steps and onto the towpath. Mark lights a cigarette and we sit with our shoes skimming the water. Camden Town is quiet and dark. Top floor office lights are still on. It's warm.

'Water and wolves,' Mark says. 'The two great fascinations of man. The two things that can hold you in awe, in naked fear.'

We light more fags and an enormous rat appears on the opposite towpath. It waddles along slowly, its head keeps diving down to gaze at the water. Mark chucks a can at it, but it takes no notice. It reminds me of the rat that ran past me in the butcher's once. I was chopping mincemeat when I heard this scuffling. I looked down and a great big rat waddles past my feet without a care. At night, whenever I hear a scuffling noise, I'm convinced it's a rat.

We walk up out of the canal and down past our house to the park. It's locked, but we find a gap in the wire. Inside there's a concrete playground. We tried that thing that goes round and round while you run with it, then you leap on and let it carry you, but this made us sick. The slide was good fun. I'd always been afraid of them when I was little, but now it was easy. Then we took turns pushing each other on the swings. It was strange, a real laugh. Higher and higher we went, in the warm night air, over silent Camden Town.

12

Let me take you back to those heady days at university. Those charming, delightful salad days. Still in my first week, I'm queuing up for dinner in my hall of residence. Groups have begun to form now, loud groups who laugh with each other, newly-formed friendships as yet untarnished. Egos expanded and nourished, for the moment content with these new affiliations.

I stand in the queue on my own, listening to the people in front and behind me. The people in front are a quiet lot. Sober dressers. Altogether they seem a modest bunch. There are three of them, and their quiet chat lapses for a bit into polite silence.

Behind me the group is loud with fake lad style chat. Clothes-wise this group is, well, high street: flash trainers, baggy sports tops, styled hair. Provincial lads.

'You should have seen yourself last night, Justin. You were well gone. Roger kept spitting in your face to see if you were awake.'

'Yeah, you poof, you spastic. I spat all over you and you still didn't wake up.'

'And then we started up our cars and bombed it down the

road. Only Roger couldn't get into his because we'd glued the lock.'

'My dad's sending me down another home-brew kit.'

'Listen poof, you should go to Saudi. My dad's got a place out there with ten servants. I only just got back two weeks ago. Me and my girlfriend are going to fly out for Christmas.'

So I thought I'd have a chat to the boys in front, the sober-looking modest lot. Introducing Ian, Adrian and Jonathan. Three pretty decent chaps really.

Ian's very British – tall, glasses, cropped fair curly hair. He wears (they all wear) very toned-down clothes: patterned V-neck jumpers, blue corduroy trousers, black slip-on shoes, diamond pattern socks. He introduces me to his two friends.

Adrian had a very strange haircut. I'm afraid it's another pudding-basin job. He has bad acne too. A permanent shy grin settles on his face. He keeps looking down at the ground.

Jonathan is very tall, a gormless look on his face and slow speech. He almost stutters when he does speak. His clothes are slightly different from the other two. A slightly sporty top instead of a V-neck pullover, even a bit of gel on his hair.

They're all from the South. Ian and Adrian from the Home Counties, Jonathan from Walthamstow.

Their politeness to me is astounding. Their quiet modest manner, their open friendliness. We sit down and eat together.

Ian does bell-ringing, Adrian collects butterflies, Jonathan likes pop music. So for an hour we chat merrily away, politely getting to know one another. I ask if anyone wants to go to the bar afterwards, but they've all got work to do.

So in the union bar that night, I sink five gin and tonics and three pints of lager. I have a satisfied look about me. Here's some people who are all right, I think. So I raise my glass in a silent toast to them. Shame they're not here, though. I think as I look around the bar, crammed full of lively groups of lads, some already chatting up girls, some already getting off with girls. I look at everyone in the whole bar appraisingly. I don't think much of them. I really don't.

So I got the bus back to my hall, back to my little room with bare walls. I put on a Northern soul tape, then some Bossa Nova. Lying on my bed, still fully clothed, I think I'll go home for the weekend.

So home I went. Mum sat in the kitchen smiling at me.

'Well go on, what's it like then?'

'Oh I don't know. It's all right. I'm not sure really.'

'Give it time, you'll settle in.'

It was good to be home. That night Mark and I went out to the Bogshed in Camden Town and had a good old dance. Lots of Northern and seventies and also this brand new sound, Go Go. Gee Longarm was the DJ at the Bogshed in those days, and he was pretty good. The Go Go stuff, from Washington DC, was new then. It sounded brilliant, although now I can't really get into it anymore. 'We need some money,' I shouted as I stomped about the floor, amongst the party people. Mark had brought this import album of Go Go. It was then the only thing you could get by this group. He also had a couple of singles. So on Sunday we spent the time dancing about the room to the new sound. To go back up to university the next day seemed stupid, irrelevant, but I had to go, didn't I?

13

'Call me Dick,' he said to the assembled students in Arts Lecture Room 1. 'I'm going to be your tutor right the way through your time here, and I want you to look on me as a friend. If you've got any problems, however personal, I want you to come and talk to me about them.'

Dick Derrick. Late twenties, OK? A real nice bloke, all right? Knows where it's at, understand? Dick Derrick, bitter-drinker. Dick Derrick, womanizer. Well, he *could* be a womanizer, you think. He tells you with his eyes that he *might* be a womanizer. You just don't know. But with a terrific guy like Dick, hell, you wouldn't be surprised, you follow?

Hey! Dick Derrick's going to be our friend! And he means that most sincerely. In fact Dick's a pretty sincere guy, right? You look in Dick's eyes and they tell you 'here is sincerity'. You look in Dick's eyes and you read the words, 'trust me'. Trust Dick, trust him, people.

Look at Dick's clothes. Tatty jeans, baggy Shetland jumper, donkey jacket. Yeah, Dick's a real man of the people. You look at him, at his clothes, and think, 'This guy sticks two fingers up at the Establishment. He can handle them,' though you smile. Dick can handle the bastards. He can play their game, sure, you laugh. But when it comes to the crunch – everyone shout this in unison now – 'Dick's on our side.'

Having had my first introductory lecture with the great Dick Derrick, I wandered around the campus for a bit.

It's a whole different world when you're on your own. You look at other people with interest and curiosity. You hunger for friendship. When you're on your own the slightest verbal contact with anyone else becomes a major event. The woman at the counter didn't say anything after my 'thank you' for the privilege of letting me buy my usual carton of sugar juice and six packets of bacon crisps. I racked my brains for hours afterwards wondering why. I blamed myself, of course. It must have been my manner. Maybe she spotted me as an insincere phoney. Maybe she thought I was ugly and beneath contempt. Did I have bad breath? Was my nose running all the time? Maybe everybody looked at me and thought 'You're not one of us. You don't belong in our world.'

After all, Tim and Joshua despised me. They didn't want to know me. The tea lady didn't want to know me. The whole fucking university looked as if it really didn't give a shit about my existence. Nobody came up and spoke to me. No girls gave me the eye. Where were all the soul and jazz fans who should have spotted me in my clothes and come gushing up to me? It seemed that clothes didn't matter here at all. Most people wore trainers and sports tops. Nobody gave a shit about button-downs, sta-press, Harringtons. Who gave a shit about London club lifestyle, about seventies and Go Go and Northern soul? Why didn't anyone come and speak to me? Why was it always me who had to make the first move, which always resulted in me being despised anyway?

It must be my fault. I'm missing something here, I

thought. I looked around the coffee shop at all the groups merrily chatting away and I felt lonely, sad and lonely, and inadequate and unwanted. Hey, you're not taking the piss, are you? You're not laughing at me now, are you? Don't. I mean, I know who gives a shit about it anyway, and all that, but even so, I mean, you've got to give people, to allow them some self-respect, some pride, or they'll just die inside.

So having sat in the coffee shop thinking desperately for hours, it soon became time for dinner. Back to my hall I went, the dear old place. I must get some alcohol for lunchtimes, for the time just before tea, and the time just after tea and before the bar opens. I went to the dining hall and spotted Adrian, Jonathan and Ian. Here were some decent people, was I glad to see them. We chatted for a time. Jonathan was going home tomorrow for a day. Adrian was going bell-ringing. Ian had started his project due in five months' time. I brought up politics, religion, music – they all responded with good replies. Replies like: 'I understand your point. I agree with several things you say. However, I'd like to take you up on this . . . '

You know, *good* replies, not filled with distrust or sarcasm, but intelligent replies. Two liberals and a socialist. It was nice. I could be flash with them and they liked it. I filled in their silences and made jokes which they laughed at. And all the time, there was no hostility, no jealous egos. All well-mannered, thoughtful people.

'Listen,' I said, warmed by the atmosphere, 'let's go down the bar tonight and have a laugh. They've got some band on.'

'Sorry,' said Jonathan, 'but I've got loads of work to do.'

'Me too,' said Adrian, 'just can't spare the time.'

'Actually, I'm not really into that sort of music,' said Ian.

'Oh right, OK, probably won't be any good anyway,' I said.

★   ★   ★

46

Yeah, yeah. You've sussed it by now. I went to the bar on my own, had a load of drinks and looked longingly and despairingly at some girls. The band was some indie job, lots of raybans, black clothes and throaty vocals. They did some really naff cover of an old soul number. 'This is soul, man, real music,' said the singer, and massacred in a jerky, clumsy white way, some obvious mouldy hit. You don't know nothing, I thought, but I cheered and clapped anyway. I'm that sort of person.

There was this group of indie types. I recognized some of them from my hall, all sitting down around a table. Later on they got up and started dancing to the band. This really naff jerky dance where they all throw their fists out and jump up and down. I wish I knew them, I thought. I bet they have a laugh, all going out together. They've even got some girls with them. I wish I had some friends who went out.

I woke up the next day at about eleven. I had a 1.30 lecture. My first ever proper lecture! I did the normal routine. Deodorant under arms. Five minutes getting the hair right. Black suede brogues today, I think, ice-blue sta-press, white button-down, blue Fred Perry cardigan, fawn mac. Two multi-vitamin tablets, followed by two raw eggs mixed in with cornflakes. Clean teeth, no toothpaste, just water. Another minute at the mirror, was everything OK? No spots, healthy smile, let's try and get a bit of self-deprecation into that smile. That's it. Surely there must be some girl out there who fancies me. Fuck, did I spend a lot of time getting ready.

Ah, sigh, reflective smile. My good old fawn mac, we were buddies. I used to wear it at school with the collar turned up. I lived in it. I bought it in the flea market in Carnaby Street when I was a mod. Do you remember the flea market? It's a big chemist now. It used to be full of little sixties shops. It had a record shop as well, specializing in Northern. A few skins used to hang out there. You always had to be careful walking down the stairs in case they spat on your parka. Many's the time I wandered around the old flea market, on my own.

Anyway, I was ready for this bastard, this toughie, this lecture, on Wordsworth no less. A poet I liked a lot.

So I got the bus into campus, da dum da dum, and I wandered around, da dum da dum. I bought six packets, da dum, of bacon crisps, da dum, and sat down, da dum da dum. I went to the toilet, da dum da dum, to look in the mirror, da dum da dum. Everything seemed fine, da dum da dum.

Five, I checked my watch. Only a few minutes before it was time to go into the lecture room. Four, there were some nice-looking girls waiting outside, so I took to my feet. Three, of course no one came to talk to me. Two, I'm pretty nervous. One, here we go, the first real lecture. The first gasp of intellectualism, the beginning.

I walked into the lecture room. There was a buzz of excited conversation from the hundred or so people there. Hey, what, big shock! Out of a hundred there were only about five boys, including me. Rows and rows of furry pencil cases and little stuffed toys marked the female army.

'Is everyone here?' asked a bored, petulant voice. 'Right then, can we all just shut up. *Thank* you. Now I'm just going to hand out these leaflets. Read them, *don't* throw them away. Jenny, would you pass these round? Thanks. Today, as you probably know, *if* you could be *bothered* to look at the timetable, we talk about Wordsworth. You've probably all done him at school and my job is to make you discard all the rubbish you learned there and look at him in a totally different light.'

At this point, the lecture room door opened and a short male student with glasses nervously made his way to the front seats.

'For Christ's sake,' shouted the lecturer, 'would you

mind terribly getting here on time? I mean, I don't expect much from you first years in the way of any academic standards.' Titters from some of the girls. 'But I do expect you to be on time.'

So the lecture continued and I, like the rest, began vigorously taking down notes on Wordsworth as understood by the professor. I really have to give myself credit for catching on quick here, because after only half an hour, I put my pen down and stopped paying any attention to the lecture. Instead, I gazed idly at all the rows of girls' necks in front of me. There were all sorts of hairstyles to be seen. Girls with pretty blonde bobs, some with long black hair that covered their napes and fell seductively on their shoulders. Some had awful frizzy messes, but some had gorgeous plaits, pony tails, bobs. Believe me, 'twas a noble view. My heart ached and a drowsy numbness pained my senses, as if of gin and tonics I had drunk.

Why did I give up taking notes on that lecture? Why do you think? Because the lecturer was a rude condescending bastard. His lecture was a load of boring crap that had probably been churned out a hundred times and written twenty years ago for his MA. His continual references to 'you poor ignorant first years' made me want to puke. The stuff he was talking about Wordsworth was sub A-level standard, delivered in a totally bored, monotonous tone. Who needs this shit, I thought. Not me.

Later on in the evening, having downed a substantial amount of alcohol, I paused to reflect on what lay before me. I thought, no, this isn't right. This isn't how it should be. I thought of home, of my family, of me, and really, honestly, this university set-up was all wrong. I thought of the past, the present and the future. I took a worldly view of the affair. This wasn't it, no way, not by a long chalk. I thought, I don't care about your lectures, your rudeness, your fucking ignorance. Inside me, there's something a whole lot better than what you have to offer. I can't really describe what it is. It's to do with profound sadness, the realization of – I don't know what.

You know, I often get this feeling, this late-night feeling. I sit on my bed and I just want to cry. I want to cry on someone's shoulder really. I want to cry on a pretty girl's shoulder. I want her to stroke my hair with a loving, understanding smile on her face. I don't want any more sadness, no more, please. No more horrible behaviour. I don't want to try to please, to be apologetic any more. I just want a girl to stroke my hair and say, it's all right now, it's all right.

14

Yo! Dick Derrick's first tutorial with us. Major *event*! Big *showdown*! Dick, I wanted to say to him, my time at school, my whole time, I wrote some brilliant essays, Dick, I was the best in my year. Dick, they gave me prizes, they did too. I came top in English. This was my subject. English took me through school. It gave me dignity. I survived because of it. I wanted to tell him this. I vowed he'd suss it – he must.

Oh God! What a waste, a fucking waste. Do you think Dick cared? Do you think he was remotely interested? But you see, trusted friend, I thought he might be. I thought he would care, inspire, praise.

What have we here to contend with? We have this.

Dick turned to one of the girls: 'So your name's Christobel, right, and you're from . . . Durham, right? Great. What sort of school did you go to, Christobel? Comp, right, terrific. And you're doing single English. Now wait a minute, you're all doing single aren't you? Well, while you're with me I want to get the best out of you. And your name's Christian, right? Where are you from then? Ah, Yorkshire. As you've probably guessed from my accent, I'm a northern lad myself. Yorkshire, born and bred.'

To be honest, I didn't really notice a strong Yorkshire accent in Dick. What I did notice was a standard middle-class voice occasionally interrupted by a sudden northern vowel, thrown in when he remembered. But still.

'And you,' he looked at me with a terrifically sincere smile – what a nice guy – 'where are you from? London. Well, well, I hope you can understand the rest of us provincials. OK. No, seriously, I hope we all get on all right.'

Yeah, just fine and dandy, I thought. Lay it on me, Dick, lay on the lit crit.

There were four of us altogether in Dick's tutorial. Christobel from Durham. Brown frizzy hair. A girl who was really remarkably quiet. She *must* be intelligent. Lucy, American, with black shiny hair. Christian, the lad from Yorkshire, with a good honest face, a sort of good-bloke face. He's all right is Christian, you'd hear in a pub. And then there was me, with my nerves and my now overtly apologetic manner.

'Now then,' Dick smiled and adjusted the collar of his donkey jacket, 'coffee, anyone?'

'Thanks,' I said, but it didn't come out right. I mouthed it OK but my voice hit a rough patch and all that came out was a croak. 'Er, thanks,' I said again.

'Yeah, right,' smiled Dick, 'OK.' He sort of half-laughed, the girls giggled. I shifted around awkwardly. I was losing things already, in the first minute.

Whoever designed the English tutorial rooms here ought to be shot. They're tiny. With five people in them you sit knee-to-knee. You can hear every bodily noise anyone makes. You can smell people's breath. They can smell yours.

For about the fifth time my foot accidentally tapped the right knee of Christobel, who was sitting opposite. This time she gave me a mean, feminine stare. A purse of the lips, an annoyed pout. I tell you, I was dying in there.

'Right then, Keats, OK. Let's see what you all know. Jack, let's start with you, shall we?' Dick leaned over to me. His sincere smile beat into my head. I heard Christobel giggle slightly. Fucking hell, I thought, I've already been picked out. I've been spotted as the enemy already.

'Yeah, well, I studied Keats at school. In fact, he's one of my favourite poets. I've always been fascinated by his poetic techniques, the way his poetry developed historically. The fundamental conclusions that he reached on life. The way he luxuriates in sensuality. I've read some interesting criticism of him in . . . '

'Yeah, right, thanks very much, Jack. Now, Christobel, what do you think of his poetry?'

'Well, er, it's very nice. His style, it's really nice. I like the way he er . . . luxuriates in sensuality.'

'Very good point, Christobel,' Dick beamed and gave us an interested and intense look. 'He luxuriates in sensuality. Very good point indeed. I want you all to write that down. Oh, you haven't got a pen, Jack. Well would you mind terribly bringing one next time? *Thank* you.'

Christian leaned over and gave me one of his pens. He had a matching set of seven – all different widths of nib.

'Lucy.' Dick gave one of his friendly looks. A look that says, 'love me, I'm fair, I'm tough, I'm cute, trust me'. 'Lucy, did you study Keats in America?'

'Oh, sure, we did Keats. Yuh, "Ode to a Nightingale", we did that. And some Shelley too, Yuh, I kinda like him, though some of his stuff is pretty drippy, y'know. But Dick, I'm really looking forward to doing him again, OK?'

'Great, super,' beamed Dick. 'I can see we've got some enthusiasm here. I want to generate a lot of enthusiasm in you all.' He glanced at me out of the corner of his eye.

'Now, Christian, would you like to read out the poem in front of you? Thanks.'

So we sat and listened to Christian read. He could have been

53

a martyr at the stake the way he read. His voice exuded goodness. His cherubic face, his fair hair, his nice manner. I could see a warm glow spread all over Dick as he listened to Christian's voice. Christobel visibly smiled at the mellifluous tones wafted around the tutorial. Lucy nodded and gave an appreciative look. Even me – I was sort of basking in Christian's glow. In the healthy haze that surrounded him, I visualized Christian in a playground, giving his last apple to the wretched, tatty, poor boy of the class. I saw him walking up in Assembly to collect his prize, whilst others' parents applauded and looked on with admiration. I saw him leading a mountaineering group on an adventure holiday, and at the disco afterwards, I saw girls look at him shyly and go 'Oh isn't he cute, I think he's really sweet.'

Yeah, you should have seen us all when Christian finished the poem. We were all sitting back with big happy grins on our faces.

'I think that's a really excellent poem. I really like the way it ends, with a sort of hopeful resolution,' I said, breaking the silence. That was a mistake, my awkward voice shattering the charmed silence left by Christian's reading. Everyone looked at me with contempt. I mean, I hated myself for it. It was just inappropriate.

Anyway, the tutorial went on, with me throwing in the occasional criticism of Keats' work, all of which were met by an annoyed and uninterested look from Dick and giggles and smirks from the girls. In fact let me describe one of these smirks. Imagine you're approached by a tramp in the street. This tramp smells badly, he has only one leg and one arm and he speaks rough Hungarian only. He offers you a piece of his pigeon pie. You say, 'No no, really, thanks very much but I've already eaten,' and you give him one of those smirks. I get them from a lot of girls, usually when I'm doing my best to be ultra-nice, to ignore any possible lack of intelligence or interesting character on their part.

'Right, that brings this tutorial to a close. Now remember, English can be *fun*. I'm no fuddy-duddy myself. I'm an easy-going type. So' – at this point a good old jokey smile appeared on Dick's face, met by some good old jokey smiles from us – 'don't take advantage of me just 'cos I'm not some old stickler. OK, great. See you then, Christian.' 'Bye Christobel. See you Lucy.' I paused, waiting for him to say something, anything. 'Oh and Jack, try and remember to bring a pen next time. And a bit more of a contribution would be appreciated, OK? Right, great . . . yeah, see you then.'

That was my first English tutorial. Something I had been looking forward to for years. Something I had dreamed about when sitting in a class full of uninterested thickos at school. So to celebrate I went out, bought a bottle of vodka and downed it promptly. Downed it just in time for dinner in fact.

'Friends, yokels, countrymen, lend me your tears,' I shouted, as I merrily sat down to dinner with my mates, Adrian, Jonathan and Ian. 'Now look, I know you guys, you lads don't go out much, I mean I know you've got a lot of work on and all that, sure, I understand that. But you know, tonight, they've got this film on at the union. I mean, who knows what wonders it might contain. It could change lives, chart new territory, heal wounds. Kids, buddies,' I looked earnestly at them. Adrian was scratching his nose furiously. 'Let's do this film tonight. People, let's go there.'

I think the film was *Superman III* or something. It was really cold in the cinema, in the main hall that had been converted to a cinema. I sat there huddled in my mac, with my scarf wrapped around me. I looked down and saw my cigarette had burned a hole in my glove. It was lonely as well, sitting on my own. In two days' time it's my birthday. I'll go home, I thought.

Home I went, with a whole burden of sadness on me. I

caught the bus from my hall down to the station. That route, from hall to the station, I mean, well, you see, it really means something to me. That route is the distance I've travelled in life, it sort of sums up what I've been through here. That road is the link between this place and home. Going down that road I can summon up all my feelings about my time at university.

Anyway, this was my nineteenth birthday, which strikes me as funny because I'm still stuck in an age-reckoning which I started when I was about seven. By now I should be a cheerful young man with the riches of the world, which would be happiness, and a girlfriend, all under my belt. Who gives you these ideas about life? Is it teachers or authors or children's TV presenters? Whoever it is has got a lot of explaining to do, to me, face to face.

The whole street turned out to a man. I was embarrassed. Lines of brightly coloured bunting, cheering, ticker tape. Even old man Riley was there – the one I used to scrump apples from as a kid. How we laughed, we sang, we drank and danced. I in my place of honour, blushing furiously. And then in came Maria, bearing an enormous cake with nineteen candles. She smiled at me as she laid the cake down before me. Maria, who I had loved since I was seven.

Nah, just nah. No such luck. I wasn't even a part of home anymore. I had left the fold. The implication was I had to make it at university. I was here only because it was my birthday. Tomorrow I had to go back. I was here on sufferance only. I spent my birthday wandering around London – the King's Road, Covent Garden, Oxford Street. I tried to take it all in, in one big breath. Something to keep me going back up at university.

15

Let me just briefly bring you up to date now. You see it's funny, but I've got this resurgence of adolescent awkwardness all of a sudden. I keep feeling embarrassed and stupid, physically deformed. Now when I talk to people, I've gone back to stooping and grinning, to total self-deprecation, to stupid smiles. Now, when I talk to people, my whole manner says, actually, I'm an awkward twat. I should be hiding behind an adult! Let me tell you, this is no laughing matter, this is, well, serious. This awkwardness is a crippling disease, succumb to it and inside you're wrecked. You become a screwed-up cripple. I can feel this disease eating away at me right now.

I know why I drink. I drink to be normal. If I *don't* drink I'm in this permanent social cripple state. Once I drink, a bit of my brain switches off. The bit that reminds me of my past, the bit that says, 'you were never loved, no one gave a fuck, so who the fuck are you, cripple?' But I was loved, I think. It's just somewhere along the line the message didn't get through. If you put me on a couch and in a trance it would probably all come out. There's definitely something wrong somewhere that goes a long way back. So I drink: *ipso dipso*.

★   ★   ★

Jesus! I was in the Bore Club. I'd charged in there completely gone on snakebites and vodka, when this nutty girl threw herself on me, literally. I'd just been indulging in a few bored, uninterested chat-ups. Actually, I was well in there, man, well in. This nutter, this crazy girl, grabbed me, she threw herself on me.

'You're tasty,' she screamed in my ear, her mad blue eyes staring at me under her tiger make-up. 'I wouldn't mind a piece of you. Come on, lover boy, let's dance, baby, come on.'

I know, I know, it's sick isn't it? It's a joke. She got me by the neck and pulled me onto the dance floor. Danced, did we? She just was clinging on to me all the time, digging her nails in my scalp, forcing kisses, rubbing up against me. Laughing madly in my face. Actually, it was a real turn off, it was pathetic – some mad stoned girl doing a big tiger-lady pose.

I mean, I suppose it was a laugh getting mauled by this girl. Getting dragged around the Bore Club by my hair. Fending off grappling hands at the bar, whilst I gave a 'Jeez, these girls, they're all over me, what can I do?' phoney smile.

'Take me home,' she purred in my ear. 'Take me home, you horny bastard,' she screamed in my earhole. She had me up at the end of the dance floor, her nails digging in my back. Well, I thought, why not?

We had to wait an hour for the night bus – that was a laugh. By then a lot of her wildcat pose had slipped. We stood still holding on to each other, the mad drunken affection now seemed a bit ridiculous. But, give her her fair dues, she kept it up on the bus, biting my ear, purring. She even bit me on the cheek. That was painful.

The night bus was about half way to Brixton when it suddenly struck me that it would be a good idea to leave this one and get off the bus in double quick time.

'Er, look, would it be all right if I got off here. I'm sure you'll be OK and . . .'

'You just stay right here with me.' She tightened her grip on my arm. 'You're not getting away.'

You know, she was nice-looking. Lovely hair. She told me I was the only white she'd ever taken back to her flat. She told me about this fifteen-year-old half-caste boy she was seeing on his days off from the remand home. She must have been over thirty, but in good shape.

'He gets me on the bed. He *throws* me on the bed. He hurts me, that's what I like.' She grinned. She shouted, 'You know, you're not my type, you're too nice. Do you know what I mean? I like real bastards. I like to be hurt. My dad? Don't ask me about my dad. He died when I was three.'

Clubbing it can be a laugh, like that. The way I do it, you really see a lot of cases, a lot of sad cases.

16

'Come in, old chap, come in. Sit down, old man.' Herb beamed and swayed about in his brogues. 'Right, booze? Fags? I happen to have some rather fine whisky about me. Ah, here we are, I think you'll like this. You don't mind a tea cup I hope? No? I always drink it neat. Chin, chin, old chap.'

Herb is my next-door neighbour in hall. We often meet each other in the corridor after I've got back from the bar pissed, and he's got back from one of his slovenly dinners pissed.

'D'ya like jazz? You do, good man. Top notch. Now, how about a bit of Fats. Fats to cheer us up, I think. If I can get the bloody thing going. There we are.'

Herb sits back and shuts his eyes. He conducts Fats as the ivories twinkle. 'Yes, that's it, that's the stuff, chap. I tell you, top notch. Positively top notch. So then, er Jack, you've got manners, not like some of these bloody uncouth chaps. Bloody uncouth, I tell you. Have some more whisky, old man. No? Still got some? You don't mind if I have a drop myself? Top notch, old chap, top notch. Now you're one of these bloody Labour chappies aren't you?

Come on, don't be silly, vote Tory, keep the bloody workers down. Jack, old chap,' Herb leaned forward towards me confidingly. He smelt strongly of whisky, but then I smelt strongly of gin, vodka, lager and beer. 'Don't you hate the working classes, chap, come on, you can level with me.'

'Herb, don't say things like that. Of course I don't, I'm second generation middle class. My parents' origins are in the working class.'

'Oh right, I see. Of course my family go way back. In fact I've actually worked out a sort of family tree.' He reached under the bed and handed me a piece of paper, meticulously drawn and charted. 'There you go, chap, how about that?'

I looked at his family tree. 'That's really nice. You've got a very old family.' I looked at his bedside table. Next to a huge bottle of whisky there were several books, all well-thumbed. There was *Class, The Sloane Ranger's Diary, The Right Stuff, History of Public Schools* and four books by Eric van der Blitz called *Blood and Death, Jaws of Steel, Panzer Division* and *Donner and Blitzen.*

His walls were covered in pictures. There were several colour nudes torn out from magazines. 'Look at that one, old chap. Damn fine girl, I tell you.' There were two large army recruitment posters. 'Brother's in the army. Captain, don't you know. What regiment? Er, the Royal Pioneer Corps. My father was in it too actually. Yes, national service.' On one wall was a huge collage of colour photographs. They were mainly of Herb. Herb horseriding, fishing, driving a tractor. Herb in a German *bier keller*, skiing, swimming, playing tennis. Herb's brother in his uniform. Herb's dog next to the family car – a Datsun Sunbeam. There were several of a fair-haired girl in a green hunting jacket. 'Ex, don't you know. Smasher to look at. Still see her now and again. Give her one occasionally, I can tell you, old chap.'

Herb poured more whisky and we sat and listened to the music. He started singing along. A teacup full of whisky in one hand, the other conducting the tape. Eyes closed, he sang, 'I'm gonna sit right down and write myself a letter, and make believe it came from you.'

'You know, Jack, I don't really think I belong in this place. Do you understand? You're a decent chap, old chap. I like you. You haven't got a smallsy on you by any chance?'

'I'm sorry,' I said, slightly taken aback, 'er, what's a smallsy?'

'You know, a smallsy, a fag, a ciggie, some tobacco.'

'Oh yeah, sure, there you go.'

'Ah, low tar. Not exactly what I like but still, a smallsy is a smallsy. You know, when I was in Turkey, they had the most fantastic smallsies. Blow your head off they would. Been all round the world, you know. I don't suppose you've seen much of the world, have you now, Jack?'

'Er, well, I've seen a bit. Of course I haven't been around the world like you have.'

'Yes, smallsies, best remedy for a cough. Damn fine invention.'

There was silence again. The whisky was making us drowsy. The tape finished. Herb rewound it and pressed 'play'.

'You know, Jack. My father was headmaster of a public school. Yes, the picture's up there, next to the one of me fishing. That's it. You see, I went there as well. Bit awkward really. Had a bit of a rough time actually. Bad idea really, sending your son to your own school. Of course it was a terrific place, marvellous smashing place.'

Silence again. The same Fats tunes. I watched Herb gulp his whisky. His hands never stopped shaking.

'I can play the trumpet, you know,' Herb announced. By this time my eyes were nearly closed. I had to peer at him through a haze of whisky, and disentangle his words from the voice of Fats. 'And the double bass.'

'He went on, Jack, old chap, I hope you won't mind me saying this, but I don't think you know much about women, do you?'

'Oh well, I don't know about that. I mean I've had a few girlfriends in my time,' I said, a bit choked.

'You know, old chap, you've got a lot going for you. You have, really. Get a bit more self-confidence in you, that's the stuff, self-confidence.'

We both gulped back more whisky and I staggered back to my room, and left him singing along to Fats.

17

Another new day at university. Another useless, insulting lecture. A carton of sugar juice and six packets of bacon crisps. Wandering round campus, checking out the various toilet mirrors. Looking at people. Another queue at dinner. More conversation with Adrian, Jonathan and Ian. Knocking back some take-out gin. Waiting around for opening time. Catching the bus in to the union. Drinks, getting the bus back, lying on my bed, reading, listening to Go Go, Northern, jazz. Falling into solitary sleep.

And then another day. And today I am approached. Yes! someone comes and talks to me.

'All right then, chum, how are you? You're Jack, aren't you? I've seen you in hall. You live just a block away. My name's Pete. Pleased to meet you.'

'Yeah, well, all right. It's really nice meeting someone, I can tell you. I've seen you about the union, you hang around with that group of indie types don't you?'

'That's right, you ought to join us, you're always on your own. Anyway, nice meeting you, come and say hello next time.'

Yo! Friends. People who go out. People who wear

different clothes, who don't wear trainers. A big group, a group of buddies. I want to be friends with these people. I was chuffed, well chuffed. Someone had come and spoken to me. Oh happy day!

This kept me going all day. I walked around with this real beamer on my face. I smiled when the tea lady spilt boiling coffee on my hand. I held doors open for people. I had *seven* packets of bacon crisps. I mean, it may seem a pretty minor event to you, someone coming and saying hello, but for me, I felt like a dog retrieving his first bone. Yeah, I felt as good as a dog, and for me that was feeling terrific.

At tea I waxed eloquent with the boys: 'In this vast and furious metropolis there are rising and falling stars. But each star shines bright, each star radiates some warmth. It does, Jonathan, I speak the truth. Adrian, trust me. Take my food, these comestibles, born of life, the living dead. Rhubarb crumble. Oh look, I'm sorry, I'm talking shit. I'm just on a bit of a high that's all.'

The boys laughed. I laughed. Hey, life isn't so bad. Come on, what are you complaining about? It's got potential. Seek it. Find. Retrieve.

A friend of Adrian's joined us at the table. An ankle-trouser job, eyes hugely magnified by his heavy-framed glasses. I do like these people, you know. I respect their modesty and self-deprecation. I admire them.

'Hello, nice to meet you. You're Jack, aren't you? My name's Damien.'

'All right, Damien. How goes it? So what do you do then at this dump? Ha ha.'

'Astro physics. But Jack, more importantly than that, I'm a Christian.'

I looked around at the boys' faces. They were all smiling sincerely.

'Oh right. Yeah, well, I was brought up as a Christian actually. You know, had to be dragged away from the telly on Sunday and all that.'

'Actually, Jack,' beamed Damien, 'I had an irreligious upbringing. My parents had no faith. It was only here that I first found salvation. I wonder, do you seek salvation?'

'Well, er, I suppose deep down I regard myself as a Christian. Yeah, sure. I mean I believe in "do as you would be done by" and all that. Yeah, I suppose I am a Christian.'

Damien gave a knowing smile. 'Ah, but are you *really* a Christian? There's a meeting tonight at seven. Perhaps you'd like to come along. I think we might be able to open your eyes to quite a few things.'

So along I trundled. Damien met me at the door of the hall meeting room: 'I'm so glad you could make it, Jack. I really am. Nick's reading the lesson. He's great. You just have to listen to his voice and shut your eyes.'

I sat down and left Damien to talk to this bloke Nick. No doubt about it, he did look a pretty impressive guy. Amongst all the ankle-trouser brigade, Nick stood out. He had carefully blow-dried hair, a smart blue sports top and ironed blue corduroy trousers. His face exuded health and goodness. Perfect caucasian regular features, not a spot in sight. I could see why Damien was so hung up on Nick.

I watched the Christian army troop into the room. There were basically two kinds. The ankle-trouser, spots and thick-rimmed glasses brigade, and the glowing complexion and sports top brigade. All had the obligatory beamers on their mugs. Some raised their eyebrows at my presence.

'I'm so glad you've come,' said one bloke who looked as if he was straight out of the *Canterbury Tales*. 'I do hope you enjoy it.'

'I think we're all here. It's nice to see some new faces amongst us.' Everybody smiled broadly. Great big happy grins. 'I'll start by reading the lesson and then we'll all have a discussion afterwards. Jenny and Roger are making the tea today, OK? Great. I'll begin.'

So Nick read the lesson. I knew this one. You probably

know it too. About some farmer throwing seeds on the land. You know, some landed on fertile land and did well. And some landed in the desert and never got off the ground. It was all so embarrassing. I was just longing to get out. You know those silences that whole groups of people have to keep up when someone is doing his speech or playing the harp, or re-enacting an obscure Chinese tragedy or something. Well, I had to sit through one of those while Nick did his stuff. The sort of silence where you suddenly become aware that you might be breathing too loudly, or that your stomach might rumble in anger.

Now when I was a kid I could just about handle this sort of bullshit, because it was grown ups in charge. Grown ups doing the service, handing round the tea. But this was people of my own age. I couldn't handle that. I mean, when I was a little kid I spotted a lot of bullshit in this sort of set up, but only with the other kids. I saw angelic little boys singing in the choir who turned into bullying little monsters outside of their surplices. At school there was a real beaut, a real peachy one of what a load of shit it all was. It was *Songs of Joy and Glory*, a television programme that screened church services. Anyway, they came to our local house of joy and glory and filmed a service. The normally seven-eighths empty church was packed out with devout worshippers. Half-way through the service the camera zoomed in on Mr Clapper, our Latin teacher. Clapper looked terrific, the ideal Christian. The camera focused right on his firm noble face as he sang loud and proud of the glories of the divine light. The camera did a zoom shot of his teeth, healthy and strong, chomping away to the hymn. Clapper was magnificent, good and fine and wholesome. A fine upstanding Christian. At school Clapper caned boys regularly. He hung around the boarding houses, bursting in on boys having showers. After I left school Clapper was sent down for two years to Pentonville. The old bugger had actually had his way with a whole succession of second and third formers.

'Jack,' beamed Damien, 'I'd like to introduce you to Nick.'

'Hello Jack, nice to meet you.' He shook my hand. It was a firm grip as he shook it. I looked at his eyes. His face was smiling but his eyes were looking at me searchingly. I read them. They said 'don't you dare take the piss, don't you dare.'

'I really enjoyed the lesson and the talk afterwards,' I said. I smiled at him and my eyes read 'don't worry, I'm no threat. Why, I might even be a bit of a mug.'

'But there's something you said that I'm not really sure about.'

'Oh really, what was that?' Nick's smile took up his whole face now. His eyes shot daggers at me. Damien looked on, smiling. The smile of the innocent.

'This bit about only confirmed Christians attaining the kingdom of heaven for certainty, and everyone else's fate being in the balance. I mean, maybe I've got it wrong or something. You see I've always had this idea that Christians believed that everyone could go to heaven, that it had nothing to do with being religious. That if you were a good person you automatically went to ... er ... heaven.'

'Ah well, you see that just isn't true. There's absolutely no certainty that you'll go to heaven if you're not a devout Christian. If however, you discover true salvation like Damien here,' Damien smiled happily in my direction, 'then you are certain of a place at God's side.'

'But what about people who've never heard of Christianity? Surely that's not fair on them.'

'Yes, precisely, that's why we must spread the word of God.' Nick's smile slipped a bit. 'Excuse me,' he said, and walked off to talk to an adoring spotty girl who had been gazing at him all evening.

Damien smiled at me. 'He's quite a guy isn't he? It was Nick who single-handed showed me the way to God's side.' His tone became earnest now. 'Jack, I think we should talk seriously about your own salvation. Come back to my room and we'll have a coffee.'

'Look, really, I'd like to but I've got a whole lot of work to do and . . .'

'Jack, this is important. The work can wait. Please.'

So I followed Damien up to his room and sat down on the edge of his bed, holding a mug of boiling hot coffee. I think I sat there for about an hour, I'm not really sure. After the first five minutes my mind switched off totally and I gazed out of the window. Damien was quite happy to talk on in his earnest monologue. Occasionally I caught drifts of what he was saying:

' . . . Nick is a true leader, a born genius. I owe my whole life to him . . . Christianity has given me strength, Jack, real strength . . . when people annoy you, when people really get on your nerves, you know, I can handle that now. You see, I'm strong.'

Time passed. Damien talked on. 'Jack,' he said, 'Jack, you must understand.' His voice was alarmingly serious now. I woke up a bit. 'Jack, Christianity helps you suppress evil thoughts.' He looked at me, his eyes wild, pleading. 'Thoughts about sex for instance, dirty thoughts. I've learned to suppress them. Those temptations from Satan.'

'Look, I'm sorry, I've really got to go.' I stood up quickly and edged towards the door. 'It's been really nice talking to you, I've really appreciated it.'

Damien looked dumbfounded, confused, sad. 'Have a bible before you go, Jack. Please, take one.'

'No, no, honestly. It would be wasted on me. Sorry, thanks anyway. See you. Thanks again.'

So I left that one, unceremoniously. I shot down the corridor and got the bus to the union bar.

I'm not ridiculing these people. Their lives are too fragile for that. I look around the bar and see a whole load of scum. These Christians, they're a notch above the scum in the bar.

I understand them. I can see why they need religion. I can see why they turn to people like Nick. I still maintain that they had a warped idea of their own religion, but I know what they mean by heaven. It represents the human dignity that you can't achieve on earth. Yeah, I know what they mean.

18

Yo! Ho! Yippie ha hoo. Guess who I'm seeing today. Dicky-boy himself. Mr Derrick. It's time for another fun-packed tutorial. It's time to rock the house. Get into gear, Dicky-boy's here.

Shit, I was late. Fuck! I'd had to queue up extra long for my bacon crisps. Cautiously, I knocked at the door.

'Come *in*, Jack! What a surprise. I thought we'd lost you.' Dick beamed, Christobel giggled, Lucy sniffed the air disdainfully, Christian just looked benign. 'Have you got a pen this time? Oh *good*. Now before you came in Christobel was making some very interesting points about Keats. Please go on, Christobel. I'm sorry about the interruption.'

'Well, er, I was just saying . . . um. That I liked Keats' poems a lot . . . because . . . er . . . giggle . . . um . . . '

'What Christobel is saying, I think,' Dick looked at me, accusingly, 'is that Keats imparts a very tangible human aspect to his poetry. Now Christian, would you like to read the poem on page four.'

Jesus, here we go.

'Sorry, Dick, but I've forgotten my book,' apologized Christian.

'Oh, that's OK. We all make mistakes, never mind. Jack, would you mind lending your book please. Thanks.'

So we sat back. Dick in raptures, whilst Christian shelled out the pearls. Then Dick talked non-stop for three-quarters of an hour on his ideas about Keats. In particular, Keats' line on class, regionalism and sex. I interjected a few observations from the criticisms I had read, bandied about a few phrases here and there. All were received in the way the Queen would receive a shrunken head from a tribe of head-hunters. You see, the disturbing thing was, Dick Derrick really wasn't a bit interested in anything I had to say at all. So after a bit I thought, sod this for a game of soldiers, and joined Christobel in her trappist-like silence. I also stopped furiously scribbling down Dick's every word.

'That about wraps it up for today then. Remember, get that essay done on Keats. 'Bye Christobel, 'bye Christian, 'bye Lucy.' Dick then began to study some papers with great interest. I slunk out of the room.

I got a letter from my mum today. She hoped I was enjoying myself a bit more and was sure I'd soon get stuck into work. She enclosed a fiver to buy a little something. She said Mark had got a job interview which looked promising. She said Charlie, our dog, was well.

I walked up to the supermarket near our hall, which was situated in a leafy suburb of the city. I spent Mum's fiver on a huge bag of pick 'n' mix and a bottle of Tizer. I sat in my room and consumed the whole lot before tea. Then I decided not to go to tea and went to sleep instead, just lying on my bed fully clothed. I woke up at eight in the evening. I read my mum's letter again. Then I went to the bar in our hall, got three pints of lager, and took them back to my room. I read *The Hobbit*, a book I always read every year or so. My mum used to read it to me when I was little. Then I went to sleep again and dreamt about home.

For a while in my life, clubbing it got quite sophisticated, seriously. Talking to pop stars, music journalists, faces about town, other people. Yeah, you know, things were OK then, just chatting away with these twenty-five to thirty-year-olds. But then it all changed. For some reason it just went back to female-hunting and drinking. But those sophisticated times, they were good, really.

Let's think. Mark and I talking about the origins of rare groove, about music politics, about art, street art, fashion. To all these older people, these journalists, yeah, that was pretty sophisticated. But then we just forsook males altogether, all that rivalry, jealousy, ego wars. It just wasn't worth it. Now that's a big tragedy, you know. That is *the* major tragedy, that males can't get along together. They just can't muck in. It's all that bloody stupid rivalry and then it's girls, dividing, felling, splitting, heating, chucking.

Take Stephano. He was a good journalist. We used to see him about in Camden Town. And at clubs we always used to talk to him. He was a serious cappucino cat. We were talking to him at clubs, right. And of course there was the usual dodgy hostility, but it usually resolved itself into friendliness. I think Mark made Stephano a bit paranoid, but we liked him. I think he liked us a bit as well. But the thing was about old Steph, his marriage was breaking up at the time and we never knew. There's us all, chatting away, all pissed up and all these tragedies being left at home to be forgotten for a few hours in a drunken loud club. It really shook me when I heard his marriage was breaking up. I mean, this was serious adult disaster. Marriage, that's really adult, that's final. Married for a year, that's all. There he was, talking to us, and all the time. . .

Bjorn Toorun, now what's that old bastard up to these days? There was another loss, another paranoid mad male rivalry scene. It always happens.

Conspiracies, conspiracies, plots, persecution. You know,

you see these old ladies in twilight homes, convinced the nurses are trying to poison them. Tramps mumble, scream, rage about plots, secret plans to get them. Conspiracies to make my life unhappy. Me, I know you see. I know this is stupid, but something smells funny around here, almost as though someone's out to get me. As though several people are out to make my life miserable, to put me down, to keep me unhappy. What sort of people would want to do this? Why, mad screwed-up monsters of course. Deranged people, trying to derange me, to get me down with them, to bring me down to hell along with all the rest.

I don't want to bring you down there, you must know and understand that. I want to climb out with you, or up to your level, or higher, but I can't get away at the moment. Hell is too vivid.

I've seen madness in people, parents, the way they scream at their kids, 'you little bastard'. I've seen it. The way teachers explode at children. The desire to bring everyone down into the very depths. Hate, despair, madness.

And then when people succeed, when they really do get to you, when they hurt you for real, violence can be about that, the unconnected sort, the sort where there's just no obvious reason. The logic, the logic of madness, behind that violence is the desire to bring the victim down into the aggressor's own private hell.

19

'I say, chap, you know I'm a pretty keen artist. Top notch, actually. Well not bad, y'know.' Herb leans on my shoulder in the hall bar.

I thought of Herb's other accomplishments. Show-jumping champion of his area, don't y'know, captain of tennis for his school, 'dab hand, dab hand,' master of the trumpet and the double bass, judo and karate champion. 'I can handle these common bastards, y'know. Just let 'em come near me, just let 'em try it.' I wondered severely about just how much truth there was in all of these achievements.

'Must draw your face, chap, really must. Y'know, I think you've got some fine features, chap, seriously. I think you could do rather well for yourself girl-wise. Have a bit of self-confidence, that's the ticket.'

'Seriously, Herb, can you draw?'

''Course I can, old chap, 'course I can.'

A few beery sports types walked past. They laughed when they saw Herb. 'It's Herbie old chap. I say, Herbie chap, how's things, eh? Top notch, old bean, no doubt. How's mater and pater? Having trouble with the chauffeur, what ho?'

'Yes, very funny, very funny.' Herb turned to me. 'Bloody uncouth yobbos. Come on, I'll get some paper and draw you.'

As I left with Herb someone called out, 'I say, Herbie chap, crash us a smallsy, crash us a smallsy for the troops, chap. Ha ha ha.' The whole bar was laughing.

'Come on Jack, old chap, let's get away from those yobbos.'

We went to my room and I poured him out a cupful of gin. His hands were shaking so much he could hardly drink. 'Ah, that's the stuff, chap. Top notch. Calms the old nerves.'

Then I sat back and let him draw my profile. I gave him a stern, sulky look. I was embarrassed. It's embarrassing having someone draw you. The funny thing was, he really could draw. His picture of me was really pretty good. I was amazed.

'Ever had a drawing of you before, eh, old chap? There you go, have it. I want you to keep it. Sort of memento, y'know.' He smiled and downed the rest of the gin.

20

Dear Jack

Please could you drop in and see me in room 102569B, about the progress of your tutorial work? Yours sincerely,

Dick

'Ah hello, come in. Just sit down and wait for a moment.' Dick reached for a huge pile of papers and studied them for about ten minutes.

'Right then, Jack, I'm glad you've come along. I just thought we might have a little informal chat about your progress so far.'

'Oh great, yeah, how am I doing?' I smiled, sitting on the edge of my seat. 'I'm really enjoying the course so far.'

'Yes, I see, OK.' Dick leaned forward with a concerned look on his sincere face. 'Jack, I'm worried about you. Very worried indeed. You don't seem to be getting into the spirit of the tutorial at all. Recently you haven't been contributing in any way to class discussions. I've noticed you don't take notes like the others. You know, it's not fair on them if you're not going to pull your weight. You have a very selfish attitude and it's got to change.'

'Oh,' I said blankly. 'Sorry.'

'Yes, all right. It's a selfish attitude that's really,' he paused and looked down at the floor, 'that's really pissing me off. Christobel, Christian and Lucy all try hard. They all contribute. But you, you can't even bring a pen to class.'

'Sorry,' I said again.

'I know what you're thinking. And I don't like your attitude at all. You come here and you think you know it all. Let me tell you, you're bloody lucky to have a place here. There's plenty of others who would be prepared to put in twice the commitment you do. I mean, I'm lucky to be here as well, I know that, and I take my work seriously, very seriously.' Dick sat back, his expression changed. 'Of course I can have a laugh, I'm no fuddy duddy. I mean, Christ, I'm only young myself.'

'Yeah, sorry,' I said.

'You know I worked bloody hard, bloody hard to get this job. I'm no arrogant young upstart. I came from a simple northern working-class background. I never had any of the privileges of London. Look, I'm going to come down hard on you. This essay due in next week, I want to see you work really hard for it. It's about time you started pulling your weight around here. OK?'

'Yeah, sorry,' I said.

'All right then. I know what you're thinking. Just remember that I know. 'Bye.'

I thought about my English reports from school. They were always glowing, always full of extravagant compliments. It's come to this has it? I thought, and ground a bacon crisp into the lino floor of the coffee shop.

21

Well, as you might have guessed by now, quite a few things were pissing me off, as Dick Derrick might say when his Mr Nice Guy image slips. To be honest, I'd hit a bit of a low. Even drink didn't seem to be helping much, even though I'd switched to a new drinking rota. This rota was supposed to minimize my alcohol tolerance level by alternating between different types of drink. So one day I'd be on gin, the next day vodka, the next lager and then a day of all of them mixed together. Some days were gin and lager days, some were vodka and lager days. But it wasn't enough, life was becoming an endless mound of bacon crisp packets.

Of course, this sort of life did allow me to do a lot of thinking. I thought about home a lot, about my family, about London. I thought about my life here too. The strange, weird set up in this place. I watched the array of different faces troop past me on their way around campus. I watched them so much that I no longer recognized them as people. Instead I saw scared fragile little egos walking around on sticks. The whole place seemed to be scared.

And my own character was undergoing quite a few

changes at the time. Yeah, I started wondering if maybe the alcohol was getting to me a little bit. I seemed to be in a permanently silent numb state during the day. Mindlessly munching bacon crisps, bloody bacon crisps. Blankly looking at the campus toilet mirrors, walking around like a zombie. I'd even developed this new walk. It was about half the speed of everyone else – real slow. My arms swinging aimlessly. But best of all was my facial expression which went with the walk. You'd have laughed, I kid you not. It was like a sleepy kid staring endlessly into a tank of tropical fish in a doctor's waiting room.

During the evening my character seemed to take on a whole different aspect. My evening begins here around lunchtime when the union bar opens. Usually I drink six measures of either gin or vodka. I can take or leave the tonic. At the moment I'm leaving the tonic. This takes me up to around two o'clock, whereupon I round off with a couple of pints of lager. Interestingly enough I seem to be the only one in the place who drinks lager. From what I overhear everyone orders things like 'a pint of Nathan's dry toadfoot' or 'pint of old Ma Rambo's special dip'. In fact if I hang around the bar area instead of sitting in my usual corner I often overhear conversations about the merits of Nathan's over Ma Rambo's.

Anyway, having finished my lunchtime tipple I'll go for a refreshing walk around campus. I've got this sussed too. There's a special smile that goes with this walk. It's a real beamer. A real grinner. I give it to everyone, even the people I bump into. I get these smiles back too, sort of amused and alarmed.

These walks take me all sorts of places around campus. I really get to see just what all these other students get up to in their work. The other day I landed up in the chemistry building. I walked in on this big experiment that they were all doing. It looked pretty weird. They all had long white coats on and were wearing these funny masks. You could only see their eyes, and those looked pretty strange.

'A mask, a mask, you must have a mask!' an alarmed white-coated monster yelled at me. 'Go to store room 42B and get one, it's down the corridor, second right, third left, up the spiral stairs and floor three in the blue lift, OK?'

'Yeah right, got it.' I stumbled about a bit looking for store room 42B, but surprisingly I got lost and ended up outside again. I tell you, I really got to see a lot of the place on these walks of mine.

At about three I'll get the bus back to hall. Then I'll sleep for a couple of hours and then go to the dining hall. My hall teas, they're a really sad affair. If you remember, I mentioned a while back about the various student groups, the clichéd categories that all students fall into. Given that the all-inclusive name for these groups as a whole is retards, the groups divide as follows: Christians, flat-tops, head-bangers, girlies, rugby players, football players, professional northerners (members cross over with rugby and football), goths, hippies, and various other minor species of student, usually lesser versions of the bigger groups.

Whoever chose the intake for our hall had superb eclectic taste. Actually, whoever chose the intake had a very sick, bizarre sense of humour. These groups were, by their very nature, permanently at war with each other. And, as is the way in wars, allies were made to strengthen the armies. Christians, hippies, girlies and headbangers joined forces against the flat-tops, rugby players, football players, professional northerners and goths.

The main battles were fought over queue-jumping in the dining hall and channel-switching in the TV room. The battles always took the same form and always had the same outcome. All the victories were won by the same tactic, adopted by both sides, the strategy of the *fait accompli*.

Queue-jumping was always won by the flat-tops. The method adopted was simple and invincible. No matter how early the Christians, etc. arrived to queue up for tea, the flat-tops would simply turn up at the last minute and walk straight to the front. Ingenious, eh?

81

Channel-switching was always won by the Christian army by another ingenious method. They would bolt down their tea in a matter of minutes and then leave *en masse* for the TV room. There they would sit in the front row of chairs and take control of the TV for the evening. Thus both sides were allowed their share of victory.

Now, where was I in amongst all this hostility? I suppose I was an outsider, although my friendship with Adrian, Jonathan and Ian put me more in the Christian camp than that of the flat-tops. But a big chance was to come about. Oh, the winds of war! I suppose this change was fairly inevitable, given certain facts about my circumstances. As you know, Adrian, Jonathan and Ian were none too keen about the idea of going out in the evenings. My fondness for going out thus meant that, well, you know, I'm always on my own. I go out every night, get pissed, sit on my own, no one to talk to. I start looking at these otherwise totally naff flat-tops and start envying their groups, their friends, the fact that they talk to girls and I'm on my own. You see it, don't you? And Adrian, Jonathan and Ian, I really like them, I mean, their morality and manner is obviously streets ahead of these other groups, but they just don't go out. I couldn't take it. I was going to sell out.

Pete, the bloke who talked to me that time, I saw him at tea today.

'All right, Jack? Join us. Sit down, I'll introduce you.'

So I sat down and got introduced. There were three flat-tops, two rugby types, two football types, three nondescripts and a professional northerner. This was a big group. In fact this was the major group in hall. These were the queue-jumpers, the beer drinkers, the trendies. I suppose I was pretty nervous, I mean, I *was* nervous. Here was I, sitting down as an outsider, in the midst of a group.

Anyway, my reception from this group was pretty good. All smiles, cheerful chat, jokes. I mean, I suppose to be brutally honest, I did have this feeling in my mind about these people. I did half think, 'Christ, what a bunch of naff twats,' but there was this voice inside my head that kept saying 'you're lonely, you've got no friends to go out with, there's bound to be more to these people than you imagine.' Does that voice ever come into your head? It's a voice with a very persuasive tone. It talks a bit like Nick, that Christian bloke. It says, 'Come on, don't be so cynical, people are nice, trust people. The world isn't so bad. Pull yourself together. Besides, who do you think you are? Who said you were any better than anyone else? I tell you, your attitude is really pissing me off. There's a lot of people out there worse off than you. Think of others. You're being stupid and selfish.' In fact, this voice sounds very like the voice of Dick Derrick, and I trust this voice as much as I trust Mr Derrick himself. But when you're down, when you're feeling low, when you've got so much alcohol in your bloodstream, you start giving room to that voice. You start thinking, 'Shit, maybe it's right. Maybe I am being too cynical, too critical.' And then it's the beginning of the end.

'It's really nice to meet you,' said this amazingly ugly creature sitting opposite me. He had fair hair cut into a severe flat-top, which made him look like some monster from the swamp. He was, I think, the ugliest person I had ever seen. But my reaction to his ugliness was one of endearment. I thought, 'Christ, you poor sod, with a face like that, I'm going to ignore those features and treat you extra special well, given all the stick you've probably taken for your face.'

'When I first saw you I thought you were the cappucino cat,' the monster said.

'Really? Thanks, cheers. Yeah, well, I like your haircut, nice flat-top that,' I said to him and smiled. 'And your name is?'

'Er, well, actually my name's a bit of a mouthful: Gonzadestum. My parents had some rather funny ideas around the time I was born. Most people call me Gonza.'

'Oh, right, Gonza, really nice to meet you.'

'And,' said Pete, 'this is Terry.' He pointed to a large fat boy who grinned at me, 'but we call him Triffid.'

Triffid nodded and said, 'All right, Jack? I've noticed you around. I like your clothes. From London are you? I thought so.'

'I thought so too,' smiled Gonza. 'Sharp dresser, makes a change from everyone else around here.'

Well, these were the first two people to show any interest in clothes, which in worldly terms is totally insignificant, but in minor terms is at least a point of interest. They both wore the standard provincial's idea of alternative clothing, in order to separate them from the casuals who inhabited their villages. Pointed black buckled shoes, jeans, any old shirt and dodgy English Harringtons. The mentality of these provincial trendies leads them to believe that hair is all-important. Once you have your hair shaved at the back and sides and relatively flat on top, and your clothes are reasonably fifties or sixties, you rank as a cut above the rest of student society. This entitles you to an unbounded arrogance over all the rest of the population. In fact I've never come across so much shallow and unfounded arrogance as with these small town provincial flat-tops.

And here I was, desperate to be their friend. Such is the cruel irony of fate. And who were the other guys in the group? What other fragile egos had bonded together in this set up? Well, there was Sonny, a little bloke. Good ol' Sonny, nice guy. Yeah, he's all right. Sonny was massively hostile towards me. Then there was Luke, who was instantly friendly with a sharp, intelligent humour. Eric, the professional northerner. 'Southern boy are you? London, bloody hell, got the smoke out of your eyes yet? It's unfriendly, that place, not like back home. Real people up home, you know. Actually I might be moving down to London after university. Get a job there.' Max, Lancashire lad, went red on introduction, sniffed disdainfully and was unfriendly. His eyes read, 'I'm no fucking poof you know. I'm not, I swear. I'm not a poof. All right, I'm a lad. OK, I like having a laugh with the lads, sure, bit of rough and tumble, you know. I'm no poof though, no way.' There was Mick, who nodded at me and said nothing. There was Jeff, big rugby type, who reached out across the table and shook my hand, and Quentin, who nodded and started flicking peas on the floor. And that, roughly, was the group.

Sitting at that table, out of the corner of my eye, I could see Adrian, Jonathan and Ian quietly sitting in their usual group, politely eating their dinner. Occasionally they would catch my eye. They smiled. 'So Jack's talking to those trendies, fair enough, I suppose we're not up to their standards.' I looked from them to this new group and back again.

'What do you talk to those vegetables for?' shouted Triffid, pointing to Adrian, Jonathan and Ian.

'Yes, I was going to ask that. Why do you talk to that bunch of retards? I mean, look at them, they're so ugly, it nearly makes me puke,' said Gonza. He and Triffid both laughed loudly.

'Come on, Jack, they're bloody vegetables, I mean, you wear good clothes, why bother with jokes like them?'

I looked at Gonza and Triffid, at their ugly grinning faces. They looked as though they were straight out of some Hogarth cartoon. I looked back at Adrian, Jonathan and Ian, quietly eating their food. Adrian took his glasses off and cleaned them. He had told me he was going bell-ringing next week.

'Look,' I said, 'I'm sorry, but people are people, they're not vegetables. They're all right. I like them.' And I looked at this new group and thought, 'you're fucking shit, you bunch of arrogant wankers.' But I wanted friends to go out with. I needed company. Besides, said the voice inside my head, maybe these provincials have got an interesting scene

85

going. Come on, said the voice, don't be so cynical, these people have got a lot going for them, and who are you anyway, nobody wants to know you. So I sat there, quiet, nervous, wanting to be liked, to be accepted. The meal finished with a food fight. Gonza and Triffid chucking peas and fish fingers at Jeff and Max. Adrian, Jonathan and Ian left and went back to their rooms to start work.

'Listen Jack, why don't you come back and have a look through my records,' Gonza asked.

'Yeah, great, I'd love to,' I smiled, and followed Gonza and Triffid out of the hall.

So there's me sitting in Gonza's room, looking through a pile of incredibly naff records, bought on the basis that the bands were indie alternative ones. The music was exclusively white, not a drop of soul. He put on some of his favourite records, hideous white voices screeching along to rhythmless guitars. Triffid sat in a corner of the room, gazing at Gonza with respect and admiration.

I looked around Gonza's room. Every item on the wall was a massive assertion of Gonza's idea of trendiness. Large black and white pictures of James Dean, concert posters of indie bands with names like The Purple Wall of Raincoats and The Shocking Guitars. The whole room screamed out a frantic message – I, Gonza, am alternative. I am not just an ugly screwed-up jerk, I am better than you. The look in Gonza's eyes held the same message. Gonza looked at me, demanding appreciation, searching for admiration.

And for some reason I gave it to him. I saw his ugly face, his screaming ego and I played along with it. It was almost the last time I was ever to feed a monster's ego. I suppose the reason was that my own was so shot to pieces.

I picked up the album cover of the record he was playing, 'My Head is a Dead Turtle' by The Shocking Guitars. The cover had four spiky-haired plonkers all dressed in black, holding Rickenbackers and standing against a background of urban decay. The band were from Liverpool, the sleeve notes told me. There was a song on the album called 'Fuck you, London'. Well then, I thought, fuck yourselves, you arrogant twatheads wouldn't last five minutes in London. Just you wait, I thought, if there are enough like-minded twats around to buy your records, you'll soon be moving home down to the capital.

I sat in Gonza's room, smiling and politely listening to the conversation. Gonza and Triffid talked on about hairspray, then Gonza showed me his collection of shirts and his pairs of shoes. His eyes searched mine for praise and admiration as I looked at the testaments of his alternative lifestyle. I smiled and praised accordingly. But there was something in my voice that I couldn't quite control, I tried, but its undertone remained. I suppose it was an undertone of incredulous mocking, of laughter. It's like I leaned over in my seat to inspect more closely Gonza's pair of new black buckled shoes which he was proudly showing me and said, 'Yeah, wow, they're really nice,' with too much sincerity, too much wide-eyed enthusiasm. Now someone with a mad, massively fragile ego is always on the look out for this sort of thing. Principally because they are so aware of their own inadequacies. For a moment I saw a light of distrust in Gonza's eyes. I saw a mad, intelligent appraisal, a frightened suspicious look. As for Triffid, well he just took my over-sincerity, my forced manner, as a joke, as an inadequacy, as a weakness, possibly to be ridiculed. I thought about Triffid. What sort of person calls people vegetables because of their clothes and appearance? Why, someone who is convinced he is a vegetable himself. My, 'Yeah, wow, they're really nice,' remark on Gonza's shoes still hung in the air. Triffid looked at me, and then smiled at Gonza, the smile saying, 'he's nervous'. Gonza thought for a second, a split second, he made a decision, and gave a complicit smile back.

They took me to a disco in another hall. I was going to be

one of the boys, they decided. You could tell this in the way we walked down the leafy road to the disco. The way they larked around with each other, asserting a two-week-old bond of friendship, whilst extending friendly gestures to me. One would walk ahead whilst the other would talk to me, about music, clothes. Then they would join each other, talk and the other one would join me in a chat. Throughout we were all smiling, enjoying each other's friendship, wanting to form an alliance against the rest of the place.

Triffid talked on to me about the people he hated in the place. They were all 'vegetables', he and Gonza had names for all of them: four eyes, spots, bizarre haircut. Triffid talked endlessly about goths, gothic punks, how much he hated them.

'Bloody plastic goths. I mean, when I came here I had all black gear on, right, the day I came here. There's these two blokes who just wore trainers and had casual haircuts. Within a week they'd got themselves flat-tops and black clothes. Bloody plastic goths, they make me sick. I was a goth months ago.'

Gonza joined in too. 'I was dressing like this months ago too. They just came here and turned trendy. Makes me sick. I mean, you were all right, you wore good clothes when you came here, like us.' Gonza smiled.

'Yeah, like us,' Triffid said.

They both looked at me. Would I join the pack, with due reservations, of course, I mean, Gonza and Triffid were buddies two weeks before I met them. I was an outsider, I had to remember that. Their look told me. But would I join them?

It was the first disco I'd been to at university where I hadn't been on my own. I sat in between Triffid and Gonza whilst they made jokes about the ugliness and the clothes of everyone in the room. Me, I was happy to be with people. I sat with my drink and beamed away. Members of their group came up and said hello. They spoke to me, they smiled! I was happy that night. I was even introduced to some girls. It was enough to be with people, to be in a group who go out and have a laugh.

22

I was fourteen and walking down the Strand when a tall man saw my face and came up to me and punched me right in the teeth. A big man punching a boy in the face. People saw of course, but no one did anything. They just ducked out of his way, fearing for themselves. And the stupid bastard got it wrong, that mental person punching me because he thought I was a happy little boy, wanting to show me real fear, the true awfulness of the world. But the scumbag got it all wrong because I was unhappy already. I was a miserable, scared, frightened child anyway.

Individual conspiracies like that are bad, terrifying, but what are perhaps more sinister, more devastating, are group conspiracies. People joining in, signing secret pacts to destroy, to kill, to maim. Group conspiracies – when you look around you, you appeal for justice and every face looks back at you with blank hostility, every face belonging to the conspiracy.

I think, I think that I might perhaps have been guilty of blind madness, that desire to bring people down into my own hell. But not terrible mindless violence, and not the sort directed at people who are not responsible and have nothing to do with my hell. I've directed my mad hate at people directly responsible for my hell. And it's always been the same reason when I've flipped. It's this mad frustration at not being loved. This desire to be loved. That's why all these mad people want a big hug, they want someone to love them. But it's difficult to give that to someone who's just beaten you up.

Yo! Do you want a cheap laugh at my expense? Of course you do, you devils. You wanna have fun? This will kill you, seriously. Imagine the scene. Me, the end of my second week at university, when I was still a teenager, helplessly in love. Aaaw, aaar. You see I wrote my feelings down at the time, on a piece of A4. Do you wanna read it? It's the genuine article. The real thing. This is exactly what I wrote all those years ago.

Stop everything – I've fallen in love. It happened on Wednesday. God knows today's Saturday and it's twenty past one in the morning. It's the most painful love I've ever felt, I'm actually pining. I'll waste away and drown in gin and tonics soon. It's like trying to swim in sand. I know she's there waiting, her drowning smile says enough. But it's that very reason that I can't make any more moves.

It's a wonderful feeling, but love does kill. For the first time ever I feel like a bleeding rose. This is not an instant and challenging love like the others, where I had to fight my way through the bracken. This is a love that I can reach out and touch across a bare room, but my hand can't move because for the first time there are no obstacles in its way. So near and yet so far, so true.

In fact I'm helpless with love, all those embarrassing phrases ring true. Head-over-heels, but my mouth and body are stone, love-sick, spellbound, all ring true. She's so, so lovely. She smiles like a waning moon. Blonde hair, and blonde hair is for gods, and there she is, and here I am, a god and a mortal. She really is as magnificent and distant as a god would be, but what hurts most is I know she's there, sitting at a table or standing with friends, and this poor dumb mortal can't even move, even when led.

How long have I got to wish, before she is snapped up by some confident chatter? How long have I got, how much longer? How long can I go on being the fool, the smiling, knowing, helpless embarrassing fool? And even now, is it too late? Saturday no longer, Sunday morning. Give me strength. Go for it. Keep on.

Yeah, I know – it's a bit hysterical isn't it? It's funny reading that now, it really was love then. It was with this girl who was head of the Jazz Society. She was quite plump with a nice blonde bob and big smile. She had a lovely big mouth and wore dinky little dungarees. I've fallen for her type before, head-over-heels jobs.

A lot of the time I'd spent going to the union bar on my own I'd been gazing at that girl, but in those days I was far too shy to make any sort of move. You know – as if you didn't know – it's a really nice feeling being in love, having crushes. I've only ever been in love four times. I'm still hoping for the next one to come along. The only problem is that if I'm in love I go all helpless, gormless. Seriously, I can't do a thing. I just get this stupid grin on my face and that's it. That's why I've never got anywhere with the girls I've fallen in love with. They think I'm a stupid moron.

Yo! You know I've got to stop saying Yo! It's becoming a disease. Yo! Shit. Stop me. Hold me back, someone, I've got to stop. Stop it now. Don't even think about it. Cut that word *right* out of your mind. Don't try it. Anyway, what I'm trying to tell you is I'm in another Dick Derrick tutorial. The Big Fun has just begun!

'Um, right, listen,' says Dick, *really* laid back. 'I had a pretty heavy night yesterday, OK. So I'm feeling a bit knackered. Now, where are we? Oh yes, essays.'

Oh shit, darn, tarnation, I haven't done mine! Why is it always me who doesn't do the work, why? Why me, damn it? What am I doing to myself? Why the fuck didn't I do it? After Dick had even called me in for a little tête-à-tête to discuss my work progress. I mean, how could I let the guy down, he was so *concerned* about me. Hey, are you smiling? Is there a good ol' grin on your face? You cunning bastard! You know why, don't you? You've sussed it. It's because I fucking well *hate* this shit. I hate Dick Derrick. I hate university. I hate fucking all this shit. But do I actually hate myself? Well, you've got me there. I'm stumped. Let's see, do I hate myself? Na, na, what, are you kidding? Of course I don't. I don't hate myself. I'm sure I don't. No, look, seriously I DO NOT, OK? But, pause, let me lean forward to you a bit and soften my tone, I do hate Dick Derrick, oh yes, I really do.

'Thanks, Christobel, thanks, Lucy. My! Christian, it looks as though you've written a whole book. Jack, where's your essay? You haven't done it. I see, would you mind telling us why you haven't done it? Would you mind explaining to Christobel, Christian and Lucy, who all managed to do theirs, why you haven't done it? You forgot! Well, well' (giggles from Christobel and Lucy). 'I see. Well then, would you mind seeing me afterwards? OK, good. Super. Now for those of us who have bothered to do some work, page 102. Christian, could you read this one please?'

I sit back in my chair and think, life's bad, life's a downer. Dick Derrick's tutorials are no fun. They're chronic. But you know what, you know what? Life's a lot worse than one of Dick's tutorials, a lot worse. Now, does that console me? You know, I don't think it really does. In fact it doesn't console me one little bit.

And what are we doing anyway? Some shit poem. Hold on there, though, don't get me wrong. I'm not dismissing poetry – Keats, Heaney. In fact, I used to write a bit of the stuff myself, seriously! In fact, I've done poetry at 'O' level, 'A' level, 'S' level. I used to read poetry for pleasure on the bus, in the park. I studied it as an art form. But now, in this tutorial, sitting with Christobel, Christian and Lucy, listening to Dick Derrick laying down the law, I don't give a fuck. How can you seriously analyse some beautiful, heartfelt, cosmologized, escapist, true and stunning piece of poetry with a bunch of people around you who don't really care themselves? I mean, let's face it, these people don't really have a lot to them. If they did they wouldn't be what they were, would they? I mean, I don't really think that Christobel, aside from giggling, is going to understand or appreciate the full weight of what's been written down here. I don't really think that Lucy is going to see just what the poet has in mind, since she thinks poetry's pretty kinda drippy anyway. As for Christian, I mean, who knows? Far be it from me, I mean Christian, I shall say not a word. And Dick, Dick Derrick, well he doesn't give a fuck about us anyway.

What are we onto now? Gerard Manley Hopkins. Knockout stuff eh? What's Derrick got to say about this one then? How can Dick possibly weave in his own interpretation of this stuff. Surely, it can't be done. I mean, 'The world is charged with the grandeur of flat caps and whippets.' I can't even see Dick trying to pull that one off. But he's pulling out some well-thumbed notes. What in God's name?

'I'd like to talk about the three main aspects of Hopkins' poetry: class, regionalism and sexuality.' Dick spoke in his sincere, matter-of-fact, no-nonsense, on-the-level, goodbloke voice. There was that little hint of artistic frustration, that slight frown, the 'Christ, pearls before swine' frown, that Dick cultivated to keep us at a subtle distance. Dick, do you know no bounds? Who are you kidding? Christobel? Certainly. Lucy? Definitely. Christian? Far be it from me to even consider that one. Me? You're not kidding me, you shit, no way. And you know that, Derrick, don't you, you bloody well know that. So have I won a slight victory here? Is it just possible that I might have got one up on Dick? You must be joking. You can't win anything in my position. I'm just a crappy student, a first year. I have no say. And anyway, Dick's sussed this. Everyone's sussed this. I'm nervous, you see. They all know that. You can piss all over someone with nerves. So Dick's safe and he knows it.

The tutorial breaks up, the girls look at me accusingly as I keep my seat, ready for a Dick Derrick agony aunt special.
    Unnecessarily Dick says, 'Right, Jack, could you stay behind please.' The look on his face is one of earnest concern. This changes to a good ol' grin for the rest. 'See you, Christobel, thanks, Lucy. Christian, keep up the good work. OK, terrific.' And now there's a bored sad look on that honest face of his. There's a 'God knows I've tried' look.
    'Jack, what's happening?' Dick gives a bewildered smile, a hurt look.
    'Er, well, I don't really know. I'm sorry about the essay. I completely forgot about it. I'll do it tomorrow. Sorry, er, look, sorry.'
    'Jack,' more severe now, 'this has got to stop. This attitude of yours, it's unproductive. It's uncreative, you're disrupting the pattern of the tutorial.' Silence. Dick gives me an intelligent look, he's going to concede something here. 'I've read your English reports from school and I can't understand it. You're obviously a person of some intelligence. Now what's gone wrong here? Take Christobel, for instance. I wouldn't exactly say she has a flair for English, but the important thing is she tries. That's what's important.'

Tries, my arse, I thought. Christobel just sits there and says nothing all tutorial. I bet her essay's cribbed straight from lecture notes and books. I mean, what's the good of that?

'I'm sorry, Dick,' I said, 'I just don't know what's wrong with me.'

'Listen, Jack, I really care about you. I'm worried.'

Bollocks, I thought, I've had this done to me before at school by my housemaster, but at least he had the grace to do it with an ironic humour, at least he half-admitted it was all bored vitriolic bullshit. But Derrick, you're something else. When are you going to drop the nice-guy bit? Now? Two minutes? Five minutes? When are you going to let rip all your frustrations in my direction?

'Quite frankly, Jack, I'm surprised and hurt by your attitude. In fact, it's really,' here we go, here we go, tell it like it is, Dicky boy, 'it's really pissing me off.'

23

Whilst lying in bed the other night I suddenly thought of a brilliant solution to a problem of mine that keeps recurring. The problem is based around this depression that keeps hitting me in the face. It's a serious problem, depression. It really gets you down.

Well, last night, I thought of this brilliant idea to help things. All I have to do is say 'I love myself' over and over again. I just lie back, close my eyes and watch all these 'I love myselfs' collect in a big black mass just in front of my eyes, just like a swarm of bees. What a load of crap, eh? What a load of old horse shit.

And while we're on the subject of horse shit, check out my conversation with Gonza and Triffid at tea today. We was well gone, man, we was well gone. Na, like I said, just a pile of horse shit. Gonza and Triffid, two fat grotesque, insecure, jealous turds. My buddies, pals, ludicrous people.

I'd totally sold out now as regards Adrian, Jonathan and Ian. I no longer sat with them at dinner. I mean, of course, I said hello, and I still liked them and all that. But I was now in this group, this group of fine people, who all went out and had fun.

Let me refresh you with another run down of the group. Gonza and Triffid, buddies in arms and flat-tops. Luke, Sonny and Quentin, the non-descripts. Pete, who goes out with Merissa, everyone calls them the loving couple. Eric, Max, Mick and Jeff, the northern sports lads.

We all sit at this one long table at tea. We all push in the queue at the start. Gonza and Triffid have adopted me for the moment. I'm being admitted to the Order of the Retard, first class.

Herb walks past, carrying his plate of food. Herb drew my picture. Herb's an artist, of sorts. I can relate to the guy. He raises an eyebrow when he sees me sitting with this group. I can read his expression exactly. It says, 'Well then, Jack, you have done well, mixing with the big group now, eh, chap, good for you, chap, jolly good.' I saw this and I wanted to separate myself from all this shit. I wanted to say, 'Herb, let's go and have some whisky and listen to Fats, it's miles better than the shit I'm in now.'

Anyway, all of the group seemed to know Herb, because they all started calling out.

'Herbie, chap, I say old bean, jolly what eh? Tally ho, Roger, Ginger. Chap, crash us a smallsy for the troops, chap, crash us a smallsy.'

'Yes, yes, all right. Very funny, very funny.' Herb shuffled off.

Gonza and Triffid lean over to me with big beamers. 'That bloke's such a tit,' enthuses Triffid. 'Yeah, he's such a pompous twat, chap. Ha ha. I say, chap, jolly what eh?' laughs Gonza.

Quentin, a quiet little non-descript, suddenly joins in with relish. 'Yes, he's such a twat. He's such a bloody twat.'

Max, the big northern lad, joins in. 'The fucking upper-class poof, the fucking twit.'

Eric, one of the professional northerners, 'Oh, he's all right though, I mean, he is a bit of a prick, like, but he's all right.'

'Yeah,' I join in, 'I like him really, he seems like a nice bloke I think.'

Everyone looks at me curiously. Gonza and Triffid smile.

'Another one of your vegetable friends, is he?' says Gonza. 'No, only joking, ha ha.'

'He may be all right, though he is a bit of a twat. But more importantly than that,' Luke, one of the non-descripts, says, 'he's a Tory, so he's obviously a bit of a bastard. I mean, his ridiculous sloane ranger pose, it's disgusting in the way it despises the working classes or anyone who's not a sloane. That's why I've got my reservations.'

People nod and grunt. Gonza and Triffid do their 'vegetable' impressions. Max, Eric and Jeff chuck bits of potato at each other. Sonny, Luke and Quentin talk. You know, there's something good about this group, aside from all the shit. There's some undercurrent of friendship that keeps us all smiling.

I try and talk to Sonny, a little non-descript. I smile and mention something about music. Sonny looks alarmed and mumbles something. Obviously I haven't been accepted well enough into the group yet. By talking to Sonny maybe I'm breaking some as yet unknown law of group hierarchy. Luke picks up my question and talks about music with me for a bit. As with Pete, I'm surprised and chuffed by such friendliness. Luke's worked in America. We talk about that for a bit. He tells me about the hillbillies who think he's a commie because of his English accent. We talk on, all smiles.

Luke's a nice bloke, I think. Yeah, let the conversation drift into friendship.

24

You know, I'm definitely getting my act back together again. I must be. You see, I'm in such a good mood right now, I'm going to tell you about *The Hobbit* by J.R.R. Tolkein. I'm sure you've read it. It's some book, isn't it? Wow, I feel good. I always read *The Hobbit*, you know, seriously. I always read it. About every six months or something, I tell you, it's magic. It's childhood all there. I'm getting carried away with excitement here. *The Hobbit* is a totally brilliant book which captures a whole load of childhood romance and lore in its adventures. There you go.

I used to read it at university loads of times when I first went there. At the end, in the middle. But I'm a bit sad now, thinking of me reading *The Hobbit* at university. Poor sod that I was. OK, OK, so I've had a few drinks. Not many though. Now there's a funny thing! How come my tolerance level has shot down of late? I mean, I've still been drinking lots but recently it only takes a few pints and I'm away. Why? Am I ill? Of course I'm ill. I'm getting older, that's it. But fuck it, I'm still young. But I digress.

I chatted up this German girl tonight. Not massively tasty, but she was all right. Got a date for tomorrow, you know. Yeah, seriously. A crucial date with some German girl who I'm not really interested in and all that. But there you go. She had a hysterical accent though, from Bavaria, but lived in Ireland. There's something about Ireland. Just recently a whole load of girls that I've chatted up had something to do with the place, not Scotland, not Wales, but Ireland. Strange.

Did you know I'm really getting better? I mean, you knew I was ill, didn't you? Or rather something was wrong with my life. I may feel a little bit better, right, but my fucking life is in real shit. Yeah, three loads of scum want to take me to court. Seriously, I could be a criminal! I owe money to a whole load of people who say if I don't pay they're going to get the law in. Bastard, I shouldn't have mentioned money. No shit, big mistake. Listen, wow, I'm loaded, man! Really, financial worries, they just aren't a problem. I'm a big success. Take a ride with me and I'll show you the lights, the big time. People know my name, they'll open doors, smile. I'll flash the cash.

Bullshit, bullshit. I don't have to tell you this, surely, you're my friend, fuck it! You're my friend and you're watching me be a major loser. I said to Mark, maybe I've Victim or Loser tattooed across my head. Mark said, 'Nah, nah, you've got Wanker up there.' Laugh, go on, I mean it is funny. But my point is that you know I'm a loser, don't you? You *know* I'm a victim, but you're still with me aren't you? You haven't turned away now, you haven't left me in the bin have you? Good. Silence. Big silence. Are you still there? Hello? You are, good. Listen, stay there, hang on, don't let go. Because . . . because . . . I've got something for you. There you go, there you have it! I've got something for you. What is it? It's . . . my love . . . my key to life . . . my knowledge . . . seriously, hang on in there.

I hope you appreciate how honest I'm being with you. I hope you appreciate it. I mean, let me tell you about a common human characteristic. It's when you're honest with someone, you admit weakness and they despise you for it. They fucking hate you for it. Well, listen, listen to me. I'm not going to take that sort of shit, no way. But now I'm getting all full of mad indignant aggression, and it's pathetic, yes, it's pathetic.

25

You know, I've discovered something interesting of late. Yeah, truly. It's that I can do successful chat-ups without much to drink, seriously. I can, it's easy. It's like jumping off a cliff. I find myself doing Mr Sincerity with ease, Mr Nice Guy is no longer a problem. And these sober chat-ups always work, or nearly always.

But we do have a problem, oh yes, just a slight problem. You see, if I'm pissed, then I can kid myself that I'm really having a good time doing these chat-ups. I can really have a chuckle. It's when I'm sober that it gets to me. It gets to me that I'm talking to these monsters, these mad girlies, these bloated monsters. I can't handle that, that I'm actually talking to them, that I have to do a massive phoney interested pose. When I'm drinking I'm not a phoney, oh no, it's all real, all that brain blanket is there, well and truly, but when I'm sober, shit, I can't handle it.

Can we talk about TV? For a moment, just a little word *en passant*. You see, I watched TV tonight, unusual for me, since I normally avoid it. It was a real struggle watching the telly, as to whether I was going to puke or not. It was bloody close, I tell you. I mean, you're not like that, are you? You're not one of those mugs, those arseholes, those hideous people on the TV. You see right through that, don't you? You laugh with me at it all. And then sometimes you get angry just like me, you want to kick the TV in, boot its teeth in, do the fucker. I understand how you feel, Jesus, it's sick isn't it? Its a sick moral joke, it's a piece of scum.

But what can you say about these TV people? What can you do? They're real aren't they and they're all over the country. Yes, these mad horrifying people are all over the place, being taken seriously, being liked, being worshipped. Oh shit! The world really is in a bad state, isn't it? What with all these TV people about, all these scumbags spewing their puke for all the world to swallow.

TV is a monster. It's a real bastard. It's shit. It's ludicrous. I mean the whole world must be mad, watching that shit. Hey, you, you bland wankers, you stupid naive people. Fuck off.

But let's talk about fishing, about the whirr noise of the reel. About birdsong and the noise rain makes on water. Let's get all gentle now, slow and gentle, and let's have a laugh. You know, I'll take you up to Camden Lock one evening, when it's really quiet. We'll listen to the gurgle of the water. We'll watch the graffiti on the bridges. We'll look at the rats on the towpath. Then maybe you'll take me somewhere that you know is special, maybe somewhere in the country. I'd like that. Would you do that for me? You see I've always lived in central London. I've never really known the countryside. I'd love it if you showed me it all. Or anywhere, if it's special to you. I'd really like that.

26

And then things took off at university. I was now part of a group. I was being accepted, things really changed then. For the first time ever I lost all that solitary wandering, all that failed ingratiation with individuals. The next person who was friendly to me was Luke.

It seems funny now, thinking about Luke when I first met him, how friendly he was, when all that sort of thing mattered. Gonza and Triffid had gone out to a disco and Luke had met me in hall and asked me round for a drink in a hall bar opposite.

When I got there Luke was sitting with Sonny at one of the tables around the bar.

'All right, Jack? Sit down, wait I'll get you a drink.'

We sat talking for a bit, about America. I can remember Luke's cheerful manner, Sonny's quiet comments, always wary of me. Look, I can't remember what we said, just that I was nervous, talkative, wanting to make a good impression. And Luke was really friendly to me, he liked me.

The three of us went back to Luke's room and he poured me a huge measure of whisky. I couldn't drink it. You know that sort of generosity, someone pouring you a huge, ludicrous measure of drink. Maybe I talked about politics, about Camden Town and the North–South divide. The sort of things that occupied my teenage school-leaver's mind.

And the next day I sat in the union bar talking to Gonza and Triffid. I said hi to Max, Nick and Jeff. Sonny nodded at me.

'Gonza, Triffid, buddies, you know, this university, it's a pretty strange set up. You look around and you start thinking, what's it all about. You know, trendiness, academic work, the whole lot.' I smiled and downed my third pint.

'You don't half talk some shit,' said Max, 'what are you on about?'

'Jack's in the clouds again,' laughed Triffid.

'Come down, Jack, come down,' said Gonza.

'No, no, what I meant was, you know, you start wondering if it's all worth it, being at this place.' I looked quizzically around me, at the faces staring back at me.

'Yeah, right mate, sure,' laughed Max. 'Hey Mick, get us a pint would you? So what's happening tonight then, Gonza?'

Gonza and Triffid talked about the parties that were going on. I looked around me for a vacant ear. Mick came back with the pints.

'All right then, er, Mick, how's things?'

'What? Oh yeah, fine.' Mick leaned over to Jeff. 'All right, Jeff, you going down the sports hall today then?'

I don't know, what can you do? It's pathetic isn't it? All that bullshit, all that bland provincial crap, that laughable group hierarchy shit. And this went on, people don't change essentially. Well I don't think they do.

I could see Gonza's keen appreciation of it all, his sharp, mad intelligence. Talking parties with Max, hairspray with Triffid, telling a joke to Jeff, passing a comment about music to me. Gonza playing the group popularity stakes all down the line, searching for status, wary, terrified of competition.

And there was the world of Triffid, cursing rivals, that same desperation for status. And Max and Jeff. Jesus, what a nightmare!

I start my specialist English course today. My schedule sheet says I've got a Dr Patsy Martin teaching me. There are two other students in the tutorial, two girls. Jenny, a quiet girl with a round, shy face, and Lucinda, a tall blonde sloaney type.

'Alrighty, nice to meet you all. I usually start my tutorials with a selection of slides of my favourite works of art. So Jenny, if you could turn the lights off.' Dr Patsy Martin ran the film.

Tutors often have these little gimmicks. Maybe they'll play you a bit of opera, or recite a nonsense poem. Often a male tutor will go on about jazz for a while. Name Charlie Parker and you can get them going for hours. I like these nice little touches. Very endearing, very human. All these things usually belie a monstrous inhumanity, but nevertheless.

By the way, I've just heard of a brilliant term that can describe Gonza, Triffid, Max, Mick, the whole lot. The term is Raw-Faced Goblins.

Anyway, in this tutorial I cracked a few jokes, made a few funnies, and the response I got, it was something else. Stony silence from Dr Patsy Martin, titters from Jenny, but the best reaction was from Lucinda, the sloaney girl. It was this incredible, monstrous, rude amazed sneer.

'My God,' exclaimed Lucinda, '*what* did you say?' She stared around the room in disbelief. 'Was that supposed to be a joke, calling one of Shakespeare's finest plays *Omelette*? My God.'

Pure, undiluted, obnoxious, revolting upper-class student disgust. There's nothing quite like it. Sloanes – what a life these people have. Debutantes, drunken honourables feeling up ladies' fishnets in little snapshots for the *Tatler*. Getting idolized by Fleet Street. What arrogance! Awkward, ludicrous people, reading about themselves, believing in themselves.

'I'd like to talk about the strong sexual undertones in Kipling's work.' Dr Patsy Martin stared at me with conviction.

And quiet Jenny sat taking notes, blissfully unaware. And Dr Patsy Martin went on about bondage and muscles and thighs. And Sloaney Lucinda continued to exist without a hint of self-deprecation or self-disgust. And inside and outside and all over the place Raw-Faced Goblins live satisfied, undisturbed lives.

You know, I saw Dick Derrick in the union bar the other night. He was with a lady, a special lady. One of the Canadian tutors over to teach Nordic literature. I could see Dick waxing eloquently away. Every now and then he would wave or smile at someone in the bar, turn back to his companion with an apologetic smile and continue waxing. On my way to the toilet I heard Dick's voice, its sincere and earnest tones, mention something about class warfare. Dick doesn't pronounce the 'a' in class like the 'a' in glass. He pronounces it like the 'a' in assassin. Very northern, very credible, and unusual for Dick too, since he manages to pronounce glass and arse in a very run-of-the-mill, middle-class accent. But then Dick's funny that way.

I saw Christobel and Lucy in the bar as well. I thought I'd go over and have a friendly chat.

'Oh, er, hello, Jack, er, how are you?' grinned Lucy. Christobel giggled.

'I see your favourite person is in the bar tonight,' Lucy said, picking up on her original disgust and anxiety at me coming over to speak to them. Christobel giggled.

108

'Girls,' I smiled generously, 'tell me honestly, what do you think of Dick?'

'Oh,' said Christobel unexpectedly, 'I think he's lovely, really lovely.'

'Yeah, I think he's kinda cute, you know, yeah, he's cute.' Lucy smiled over at Dick. Dick gave a matey wave back, but frowned and looked uneasy when he saw me. Cute, I thought. Jesus, cute, I mean, what can you do, what *can* you do?

I often wonder, with these old male tutors, the cute ones, the ones who do the father-figure bit, I wonder how many of them actually get their wicked way with these dumb girls.

27

I can't help getting the feeling that some of you are starting to think that I have a fairly cynical outlook on life. Maybe you think I'm the sort of person not to bring to parties. Even that my views on life are not very 'nice'. But, hey people, you couldn't be more wrong. Seriously I'm a really good guy, dead polite, charming, friendly in the extreme. Believe me, friend, please believe me. I'm not begging, I'm not, it's just sometimes it all gets a bit much, you understand, don't you. Christ! Do you understand, maybe you don't. So is it up shit creek without a paddle? Well it always was, I suppose.

No no no. Today I have complete confidence in you. I rest assured. Can I get all sentimental with you again? Of course I can, you sly old foxes, you. I've written this little poem that I want to share with you. It's really shit, right, but, BUT it really sums up what it was like waiting for the bus after watching a film in the union building one evening.

> The snow began to fall last night
> While I was inside watching the film
> It fell as I stood outside, light
> Fell softly down as we queued to go home

The bus came steaming up the hill
I sighed with the rest to be out of the chill

Er . . . there you go. But it *is* sort of nice isn't it? I've almost forgotten about those sensual experiences of nature, cold, warmth, all that sort of thing. I wonder if that's the answer to it all, to forget all that human shit, and just start getting into nature's sensual delights. Sunsets, foggy mornings, that sort of thing.

But at university the reality is Gonza and Triffid, Max and Mick, Dick and Lucy.

Dick Derrick's next tutorial is imminent. It occurred to me that there might conceivably be room for me to introduce a bit of irony into the old tutorial, to get Christian laughing, to shock Christobel and Lucy, to infuriate Dick. Why not, why the fuck not, get that scumbag on his toes? But how to play Dick at his own game. I've got it! I know, that's how I'll get him. It means time and effort admittedly, but it's worth it.

But first, an evening in the company of Gonza and Triffid, delightful. Triffid seems to be after my jacket. He keeps going on about how it doesn't suit me.

'It's not *you*, Jack, it really isn't. Now those other jackets you've got, they suit you, but not that one, oh no. Actually could I try it on, you know, I think it looks pretty good on me. It really does, doesn't it, Gonza?'

'What? Oh yeah, really good, ha ha.' Gonza smiles and goes to dance to some shit song that's playing. Triffid follows close on his heels. I follow them too, and we dance in a circle, passing round a pair of Raybans. I'm really trying to get into the spirit of things, you know. I keep telling myself, these are my friends, my good friends. I've developed a special beamer for this. The only trouble is it makes my nose twitch. It's the effort, the strain. My face is taking the piss out of me.

111

And the big news is, Sonny's starting to be friendly to me. Sonny, the quiet, suspicious one, the one who gives me terrified looks whenever I try to speak to him. Sonny has obviously made a conscious, well thought out decision, and weighed me in the scales of group hierarchy and has found me now acceptable to talk to.

I'm flattered, you know, I'm positively choked that Sonny has decided to talk to me. I'm really choked up about it. He talked to me at lunch-time, luckily I hadn't had too many pints so I wasn't going to do my philosophical bit, always a bad idea. Keep the subjects on music, sport, anything acceptable. Never venture into the realms of intelligence. People just won't stand for that sort of thing.

I tried desperately to search for common ground. Politics, yes, CND, yes, music, hey! Sonny liked sixties stuff, not soul but pop, but still. We were in a good era. So me and Sonny rapped awhile and I do believe that Sonny was pretty choked himself, what with me being so overtly friendly, what with me making such a big effort to get on with him.

'Er, listen, Jack, do you want to go to the union bar tonight, have a few drinks and all that?'

'Oh, thanks, Sonny, that would be great. See you at eight.'

Well how's about that then? Sonny is a very good friend of mine. I spent the day thinking about what topics to bring up in the bar. Steer well clear of soul music, that's an obvious dislike with old Sonny. Don't mention anything to do with height. I know, do a massive, titanic, self-deprecation bit, that's bound to go down a storm. I can see it now. Yes, Sonny, me too, I had no friends at school. Yes, I share the same disgust at sports-types, bullies. I'm also hung up on that school hierarchy bit. I had the whole evening planned and sussed.

Before I saw him that evening I thought I might try some of that stuff I'd got, for a laugh. I thought it might make me a

112

bit more lively company for Sonny, maybe it would give me a few in-depth insights on life that I could pass on that evening in conversation.

So I locked the door of my room, it was very exciting. I unearthed this stuff and got it all ready to take. When I bought it I was told it was well powerful, but you never believe all that shit these hippies give you, these small businessmen.

I smoked a whole paper full, and sat back waiting for something to happen, but nothing did. So I rolled two more, I put in everything there was, because I thought it must be pretty weak stuff. I smoked those two really quickly, inhaling it all deeply, because I remembered I had to meet Sonny in ten minutes. I still hadn't noticed any effect, until I tried to stand up. It seemed to take ages, and when I got up I'd grown about four feet. I hovered around the room a bit and then sat back on the bed. I looked around lazily, wearily. There was a fire going on right next to me, this last joint had set the sheets on fire. I looked at the orange and yellow flames for a bit. Then I thought I'd better put it out. This took quite a long time, it seemed like hours actually, but eventually I got the fire out.

I walked out of my room. I passed Pete with his girl-friend, Merissa, in the hall.

'All right Jack, how's things?' Pete smiled. I just stared back, I couldn't say anything.

Sonny was waiting at the bus stop. It's so ludicrous this, Sonny was still in his 'yes, we've just met and decided we have things in common, let's talk some more about self-deprecation and sixties pop' frame of mind. That's how things should have been. But me, I was completely gone on drugs, I didn't know *what* was going on. You know, in a way, I think I beat time at its game then, I pre-empted a whole lot of hours 'getting to know someone'. Well, obviously I didn't beat anyone and the whole thing was pretty sad and pathetic. But, sod it, at least it stopped all that

113

phoney friendly bullshit, at least Sonny had dumped on him some doped-up case.

When you're sad, you're vulnerable, you see things in a different light. I remember meeting Sonny then, but in a different way. You know, it was such a nice feeling to have friends then. University was magic, seriously, but I've forgotten that because of what happened there later. But it was really magic, walking down the corridor, feeling ten foot tall. When I saw Pete, I wanted to say what a good bloke I thought he was. It was all magical, all these people, all talking to me.

It was in that frame of mine that I met Sonny, it was in that frame of mind that I met everyone, completely magical, innocent, I was a really sweet boy, it's touching thinking about it. I sat on the bus with Sonny completely out of my head, going on about how slow the journey was, how big the trees looked. He kept asking me what I was on, I wouldn't tell him. He must have thought I was a complete weirdo. Poor old Sonny, he just was the sort of person to end up with a drugged-up case. I can imagine what he must have thought but, hysterically, this incident boosted my group hierarchy points incredibly, it gave me a respect and popularity I'd never dreamed of, and it also sparked off more events that were a laugh, a real laugh.

I was sitting in the bar with Sonny in an utterly paranoid state. I started seeing beetles and lice crawling all over my body, eating my arms and legs, I thought I was going to die. I kept saying to Sonny 'It's all right, it's all right, I'm going to survive, I'm going to be all right.' But I kept thinking I was going to die. I kept gazing around the bar at people's faces. Faces I had seen every day, well now they were looking at me, out of my head, I wonder what sort of screwed-up, inhibited loner they thought I was. And then I felt all guilty, a real hangover from home and school, I felt terrible. I felt guilty about Sonny, I kept apologizing. My legs couldn't keep still, I kicked the table and knocked over

114

his pint. Then I got better, during the evening. I don't know what was in that stuff, but it was pretty strange. The point is, maybe, that it got a bit of the irrational guilt and fear out of me. The stuff you have inside you when you're inhibited, the lack of self-confidence. The sort of state millions of people are walking around in, maybe it's quite a big teenage thing. Anyway, if any good came out of that situation, which it did, hopefully, I lost a bit of that guilt and fear. Because, you know, that's what a lot of my initial time at university was all about, losing that guilt and fear. That's what that group was all about, as well, every single member, all trying to get better. And now I realize we all did grow up and lose it, in our time there, but what happened to us all? We liked each other, we were all friends, really, so what happened?

Sentiment, ah! Sentimental visitations, how sweet they are, gentle, languid, momentary. It's so difficult for sentiment to last in a largely unsentimental world, you have to take it as a luxury good, savour its sweet charm and lock it away again.

28

It was one of those sunny Sunday mornings when God smiles down on his people and it makes you feel good walking down the street. I thought to myself, it really would be nice to appreciate once more the quivering dew drop on the hawthorn branch. I thought perhaps that I might be getting back together again.

You know, lots of things happened at university, all those few years ago. Things that I'm still trying to recover from, as it were. I mean, it was nothing too dramatic, nothing really incredible, but it was a pretty bad experience. For instance, walking around the market today, I saw a couple of ex-students from old Turd Hall. I walked past them and, well, it was all a bit pathetic really. And then I saw this girl who I used to be in love with, and we ignored each other. And then my hair went funny, a big curl suddenly appeared and wouldn't go away and that was pretty ridiculous. Everything was STUPID and it shouldn't be like that now, should it?

Sunday afternoons, they really force you to come to terms with yourself, don't they? It's like someone dragging you out of bed by your hair and forcing you to look in a mirror. I think the really big questions arrive on Sunday when families have outings and couples try and get on through the daylight. Sundays are bad, your mind wanders.

Sometimes I feel I ought to get sentimental about Camden Town, after all, I did grow up here, for the last ten years. But I can't, it doesn't seem to merit it. It's just a collection of buildings, a tube, a canal. At weekends it's a tourist attraction and belongs to a whole army of people. It's not a place that you can really love and call your own, principally because of the market. I tell people where I live and they say, 'Oh yes, we go there all the time, to the market.' And that makes it a bit of a joke really, how can I claim to have any real identity with a place that prostitutes itself so much?

Phew I've got a cold! A real stinker! A real stonker of a cold! Now here's something we can all agree on, something that will touch all our hearts deeply. The agony of blowing your sore red nose into a used wet tissue. Ooh! Painful isn't it, just think of it. Sometimes it's nice to have the odd cute little chat, the occasional, 'know what you mean, oh yes, ha ha, know what you mean,' cosy, cosy, cosy. Chalk on a board, road drills, breath in the morning, all these things bind us together, little human quirks, they bring us all into a common bond of sympathy and understanding. But if I said something about social anxiety, madness, suicidal depression, I don't think I'd get the same sort of reaction. There wouldn't be any 'know what you mean, of course' little remarks, would there? Perhaps there'd be alarm, fear, awkwardness. That's a shame isn't it. Because these things, the things we all secretly dread and suppress and hide, they're as universally felt as sore noses.

Fear, weak human fear, the desire to hide and pretend it didn't happen, out of fear, and the injustice and the general poverty of intelligence. I walk around Covent Garden and watch people stand and applaud the magicians and comedi-

117

ans. I see them appraise the humour and the remarks. What I'm trying to say is Covent Garden reminds me of an American TV series. It's full of break-dancers, saxophonists on skateboards, wise-cracking magicians. It's full of advertiser's images of how life should be. You stand and applaud the break-dancers. 'Hey, like it, I like your style, very youth, very young. And youth is good, because youth is innocent, right?' And then you see them bringing little kiddies into the act and you think, 'Hey, like it, racial harmony, beating the age gap, that's good.' Then you watch the saxophonist on his skateboard and you think, 'Hey, like it, what a cool guy, really smooth, that's cool, I respect that.' And then you stand and watch the magician and laugh when he makes a joke about your check trousers or your zoom-lens camera and you respect him for his humour. And before you jet off back home you think, 'Hey, I like it.' And your view of life ends up consisting of a stream of misconceptions and misunderstandings. And then you teach your kids all the wrong values and screw them up and they all die of heroin overdoses. And then you die and get buried in the family plot and your wife starts sleeping with the orthodontist or the osteopath. Nobody really cares and you got it all wrong anyway. And your name could be Hank Willbemeer the Fourth, or something, and you only really ever loved and were loved by your dog, Zonk.

What I really wanted to tell you was that I'm going back up to university for a day. I'm going back up to reminisce, to think about the old days. I plan to wander around the town and the campus to get the feel of it all again. I'll let you know what it's like to be back, just for a day, after all this time.

29

Ha! Dick Derrick's tutorial! I had it planned, I had it sussed, simple, yet brilliant. In the few days before the tutorial I had worked my arse off preparing for it. Every piece of criticism I could find on Lord Alfred Tennyson, I'd dug up and scrutinized. Everything. I could have done an MA on him that day.

'Hello Christian, hello Christobel, hello Lucy.' Dick sat sincerely smiling at us as we walked in, his donkey jacket hung prominently on the back of a chair.

'Hello Dick, lovely weather,' I beamed as I sat down. 'I've really been looking forward to this tutorial.'

Dick looked unnerved, startled, suspicious.

'Oh yes, good, I see you've actually got a book with you this time, Jack. Turning over a new leaf are we? Ha ha ha.'

Christobel giggled, Lucy smirked, Christian . . . well, far be it from me to say what Christian's reaction to this new approach was. Serene? Inscrutable?

'Now I'd like to talk about the three main aspects of Tennyson's work.' Dick leaned forward in his chair and gave us a severe, intense look. 'I'd like to talk about class, regionalism and sex.'

'I'm glad you mentioned that, Dick, I'm sincerely glad. I've read some interesting criticism on this and I've come up with the following . . .

Well basically, I spent the whole tutorial reeling off a whole load of stuff. I totally monopolized the tutorial. No one could get a word in edgeways. Dick was getting more and more irritated. That was a pleasure to watch, but basically, in all honesty, it was a pretty futile exercise. That's the thing, you know, you just can't win with these people. These scumbags. It gave me a bit of satisfaction, but not much, not really.

After the tutorial I sat in the bar, stuffing down bacon crisps when Gonza and Triffid came gushing up to me.

'Jack mate,' called Gonza cheerfully, his eyes bright, 'I hear you've been puffing away at the old stuff then.'

'Yeah,' said Triffid, 'according to Sonny, you were out of your head.'

'Well, er, maybe I got a bit out of it, guys, I was a bit out, yeah.'

'Of course,' said Gonza, 'I've done loads of stuff, you know. I do it all the time. Only the other day me and Triffid got completely out of our heads, didn't we, Triffid?'

'Oh yeah, yeah, that's right. We've had loads in the past few weeks.'

Then Luke came lolloping up.

'All right, Jack? I hear you were a bit out of your head the other day.' He smiled knowingly and walked off.

Gonza and Triffid talked for a while about hairspray and how much they hated plastic goths. After a while Triffid went off and I was left with Gonza. 'I see you're wearing a polo-neck jumper. Is that supposed to be trendy or something? Listen, I've seen loads of real squares wearing polo-neck jumpers, I don't think they're trendy at all,' Gonza sneered.

Jesus, that was frightening. I could see right through

120

Gonza. See his terrifying jealousy and hate, his massive horrendous ego. It was all revealed. It was horrific. You get these sorts of monsters all over the place, you know. They survive in groups, groups are their life blood, their whole existence. Watch out for them, beware. But then, while I was gazing at Gonza with incredulity, that fucking stupid voice came into my head again.

'Listen mate,' it said, 'just who do you think you are? So the guy's a bit of a bastard, but there must be more to him than that. Don't be so cynical. You criticize too much and who do you think you are anyway? People are nice, give them a chance!' That voice, that naive little voice, keep it at bay, keep it at bay. But what did I have, a shit boring life here at any rate. No solace to be found in academic work, loneliness, drink. So I let it slip. I gave Gonza another chance, the benefit of the doubt and let it slip.

Max and Jeff came up. 'All right, Gonza, what parties are on tonight then?'

I sat for a while in numb silence, got another drink, sat and listened. Then I got up and went for a walk around the campus.

You know what, you revolting scumbags? I was born for greater things than this. I was born for better things than sitting in the pub, taking a load of crap from shitheads. I was born to a magnificent tradition of supreme thinkers, architects of the mind. How can I talk to you, you bland turgid twats? I don't know.

I tell you I was super wise when I was a little tot in primary school. Yeah, when I was little, I knew all about dignity, humility, sadness, grace, real beauty. That world does exist, and you shitheads deny it. You deny it me by your crap, shit lives. You scumbags must laugh, you people, because I had it all taken away from me, when I was just little. Yeah, just before I realized, before I could really get to grips with things, I had it all taken away.

121

So now, there's nothing left, nothing. No love, no fuck-ing love. And that's why I'm all washed up. No shit, I'm wasted. One big fuck up. You know what, listen, I'm going to tell you something really real. Something that's just fucking it. I could have made it with a bit of love. That's all I needed, just some love to keep me together, to stop me falling apart.

Anger gets you like that. Real anger. Anger at people and their disgusting ways.

30

I sat in my hall room alone, bored, thoughtful. I thought, 'I think I'll try and forgive my dad.'

I had these really nice jazz chords already worked out on the guitar. I put words to them. I remember once he'd told me about the day I was born and how he wandered around the park afterwards. So I wrote this, and it sounded really nice with the chords.

Cast your mind back to an autumn in the sixties
When the leaves were turning yellow and falling from the
    trees
A figure in the park looking strangely unfamiliar
[pause for chords]
Many years later you tried to tell me how much you care
That walking in the park you felt that you were walking on
    air

Those words seem like the purest form of poetry
They were among the nicest that you ever spoke to me

That's how I forgave him, thinking of that, trying to re-member something long ago. Just that picture of him. Sentiment, sweet sentiment, that ironic invention.

Do you hate your father?
Yes, yes, I do hate him.
Why?

Because it's all a falsehood, because he told me he was having an affair with some scummy slag before I was ever born. So it's all a joke, me trying to piece it all together, thinking of him as family, when all the time, before I was even born, his dirty greed and immoral nature led him to sacrifice my family. Because of what he did to my mother, the hurt she suffered.

The indignity, the sheer bloody indignity. I hate him. All along he never was true to my mother while I was born. There was never a moment in my life when my dad was true to my mother. And there's me trying to forgive him and trying to work out in my mind some bond with him, something to love him for. When all the time he was a liar and a cheat, a greedy deceiver. I remember his kindness towards me though. I remember that. I remember loving him, that's why I tried to forgive him then. But it's all a falsehood.

I think of him and the slag he ran off with, together now in their sordid deceitful relationship, and it makes me want to vomit. May you rot in hell, you worthless scum.

31

Today at university, I got a postcard from an old school friend, Haram. It appears he's having an interesting time doing computer science in Margate. That's nice. I'm too depressed to write back to him though.

Old school friends, I wonder how they're all getting on. I don't suppose I'll ever have much to do with them anymore, not after the different things that we're all going through.

I met Steve in the summer holidays after 'A' levels. He hated me, I really revolted him. Christianity can do that to people. He's so screwed up about it, his religion. How embarrassing for him to be a Christian. I wonder when he'll stop believing. Get out of suburbia, my boy, out out out! I tell you something, that's pretty sad. He's now too embarrassed to see me. Why? Because the last time I saw him I was a wreck, knocking back the pints, a real loser. Drunken losers like me, they tend to embarrass people.

It was only after leaving school that I realized what a wanker this bloke was. What a jerk. A lot of people didn't like him at the time, come to think of it. His crawling to the school system, his taking all that discipline seriously. I

125

remember him taking me to one side and saying, 'Jack, our housemaster's asked me to have a word with you.' I mean, fucking hell! There was some inferior jerk patronizing me for the sake of some ludicrous bullshit school rules.

For a time at school my best friend was John, but he left in about the fourth form. I remember when I was invited over for his birthday. God that was sad. He had an older hippy brother and a mad mother who treated him like total shit. We went round the Barbican and some old streets of London on one of those specially planned tours. A typical olde-worlde middle-class thing to do really. Almost touching in fact. We were in some church, me, John and his mother, admiring the stone-work or the stained glass or something. I said something funny to John and we both started giggling.

'Get out,' yelled his mother, 'get out you little brats, you little bastards!'

We sat outside the church waiting for his mother to come out and forgive us. The look on John's face, his eyes just stared ahead, and I couldn't say anything. And it was his birthday.

I remember John's older hippy brother. He always used to come down when we were playing subbuteo. He'd make fun of John, openly bully him in front of me.

Once when his brother had left the room, John smashed up all the red subbuteo players because they were his brother's favourite colours. The thing was, it was John's own subbuteo set, but he still smashed it up. He wouldn't have dared smash up anything of his brother's.

He always had a red blotchy face and he always smelt. His mother never washed any of his clothes and everyone at school said he smelt. Another funny thing about him was his fascination for food. He'd spend ages eating a small bar of chocolate, he loved talking about food. His mother never fed him either. He was as thin as a rake. I'd go round there and there'd be nothing to eat in the whole house. He and his

126

brother used to stay up till ten o'clock each night, waiting for their mother to come home and give them money for chips.

And they were a wealthy family as well, their mum had some top job in an advertising agency.

I remember going down with John to the living room where his mother was sitting with friends. The room was full of cigarette smoke and arty middle-class voices laughing. John asked for some money for chips.

'Oh, really, Jenny, why do you let the kid bug you all the time? Tell him he can do without chips for once, the greedy little monster!' a laughing woman's voice shouted.

Then for three weeks John never turned up to school. So I went round to see him. His mother answered the door.

'Oh, it's you, is it?' she said with distaste. 'John's upstairs in his room. He got what he deserved. It was his own stupid fault. I've got no sympathy for him.'

I went up to his room, he was reading his adventure comics. Across his red blotchy face was a huge scar, all done up with stitches.

'My brother did it,' he said, 'we had a fight and I got this knife from the kitchen to protect myself. I thought that if I had this knife, I could run upstairs to my room and lock myself in without my brother beating me up on the way. But he was waiting for me at the top of the stairs. He cornered me on the staircase. He kept kicking the knife hard so that it was going nearer and nearer my face. I begged him not to but he was laughing and he just kicked harder and harder and it got nearer. And then he gave a really massive kick and the knife went into my face, it stuck there as well. When Mum came home he said it was all my fault. She never asked me about it. You see she doesn't care.'

John never went back to school. I met some people who knew him, a few years later. Apparently his mother kept locking him out of the house so he had to sleep in the street. Then she kicked him out altogether. He lived in some squat and now he's in prison for stealing. Apparently he's heavily involved with heroin.

Hell, don't be so cynical, people are nice, look on the bright side. Mad monsters, what are you talking about?

'I wear slit skirts, Jack, I like to look feminine, attractive.' She showed me, she showed me her slit skirt. This is my specialist English course tutor, Dr Patsy Martin. We are alone together in the tutorial. The other two girls haven't turned up.

'Women have strong sexual desires; some like to be hurt, some like to be treated gently.' She smiled and looked straight at me.

'My Michelangelo nudes for instance,' she said, and we both looked around the walls of her room where they were stuck up, 'many women find strong muscular bodies sexually magnetic.'

There was a long pause while we both reflected on this. Then she reached into her bag and pulled out my essay. It was covered in her red ink. She held it distastefully by a corner.

'Jack,' her tone suddenly shrill, 'when I was at university if I handed in a piece of work like this I would expect to be reprimanded most severely. You ought to be ashamed, ashamed to have written it. There's no double margin, you've put "Mrs" instead of "Dr" Martin, your writing's untidy, your sentence structure erratic. It's too short, and you haven't read any of the articles I've written. It's a sloppy piece of work.' She paused to catch breath. 'You want me to show this to the head of the faculty because that's just what I feel like doing? I could see you punished for this you know. I suppose you think you're some sort of bigshot with your fancy ideas and your flashy clothes. Well, let me tell you that there are a whole lot more people here prepared to put twice the effort you put into work. The two girls in the tutorial for instance, they work far harder than you do.'

128

'Actually,' I said sincerely, because in sincere situations like this you've got to be sincere, 'I was wondering where the girls were.'

'Right, OK, well I understand that Jenny is feeling ill and Lucinda has a lot of work on and so can't make it.' She paused again. 'Do you have any personal problems, Jack? Anything that you want to tell me.?'

'Er no, I'll all right, thanks.'

'My husband, we work hard at this university and we, I, expect hard work from my students in return. I don't think there's any point in continuing with this tutorial. I think we'll call it a day.'

I shuffled out of the room.

I saw Gonza and Triffid at lunch today. Gonza was wearing a brand new polo-neck jumper. Apparently psychopaths have no guilt: Raw-Faced Goblins, greedy monsters, they have no shame.

Luke came up to me at lunch as well.

'All right, Jack? Do you fancy doing some hot knives tonight, then?'

Now what the fuck was hot knives? I didn't have a clue but the way Luke was talking to me presumably meant I should know.

'Yeah, great, hot knives. Love to.'

So that night me and Eric, the professional northerner, sat in Luke's room and watched him take out a gas burner and all this other stuff. It was good fun really. I sat with tears streaming from my eyes, coughing in the lungful of smoke. Eric's face started going into ludicrous contortions that seemed to match his personality. He turned into a garden gnome at one point. He was pissing himself at me, so presumably the same thing was happening with him.

Through a lungful of smoke, my eyes streaming with tears, I wanted to tell Luke that I'd never had any real friends and that I hadn't really known what hot knives were and

129

that I was really sad when we moved house when I was little. But we didn't say anything in particular, we just sat and smiled and then left. I went back to my room, walked about a bit and was happy.

A couple of encounters today. Firstly I met Christian in the bar at lunch. Dick's golden boy, the apple of his eye. I asked him what he thought of Dick's tutorials.

'Dick Derrick,' Christian looked around him dismissively, 'he's a wanker.'

You know I was starting to enjoy university, things were picking up.

Secondly in the bar this evening, this bloke Tom came up to me. I didn't really know him, just that he was from London and looked quite sharp.

'You hang out with Gonza and Triffid, don't you?' He looked at me curiously. 'What are you hanging out with them for, they're scum.'

I downed my eighth pint and smiled at him. 'Na,' I said, bless me, 'na, Gonza and Triffid are all right, they're my friends.'

He looked at me, shrugged his shoulders and walked off. I got in a couple more pints.

Oh yeah, today I heard some sad news. Herbie, you remember Herbie, he's left, he's quit. Apparently, he'd missed all his tutorials and was massively in debt to the bank over drink bills.

Hot knives at Luke's started to become a regular thing now. The whole group would sit in on the sessions. Eric did these brilliant Herbie impressions, how we laughed! I talked happily away with Pete. He seemed like a good bloke, Merissa like a nice girl. Everyone said how devoted they were to each other.

I'd wake up at about twelve. I didn't go to any lectures at all by now. I'd go into the union bar and have a couple of pints and some lunch, talk to whatever members of the group were about. Then I'd go back to hall and push in with the others in the dinner queue. After dinner we'd go out to a pub or a hall bar. This was the worst time really. Actually having to make conversation with different members of the group. All the time observing the poxy status of its members, watching people being forced into roles – all that bullshit. Then on to a party or a disco, where I sought for the perfect girl but never found one. The ones I really liked I was just too shy to talk to. And then back to Luke's for hot knives. The knives sessions were getting more and more hysterical the more we had. We even started doing them on the hall's kitchen stoves. Just pissing ourselves laughing for ages. And I started getting to be good buddies with Sonny and Pete and Quentin.

Sometimes, during the time after lunch and before dinner, I'd go up to the supermarket near our hall. It was brilliant, a massive place that sold everything. Honestly, going there was brilliant. I'd dodge about with a trolley, buying loads of pick 'n' mix and Tizer. Then I'd go back and scoff it all.

I remember one night of knives very well. We'd all got totally out of it. I went back to my room and just danced all round the floor. I kept putting on this record Sonny had got me into, this indie band. I just danced and danced for hours. I danced in front of the mirror. I looked at myself and I said 'It's all right now, it's all right. Your worries are over. It's all right now.' And you know what? That day, that *delirium* was the happiest and best day of my whole life.

It was nearly Christmas, the local supermarket had its decorations up, plastic Santas and big 'Happy Xmas' signs. I'd bought a little silver Christmas tree and lights for my room. Members of the group would be ushered in to see it, that was a laugh.

We organized a big Christmas meal with turkey and all the works. I even donated my Christmas tree for the room. There was loads of drink. We all sat around smiling, out of our heads, a celebration of friendship.

131

32

Now, when the world seems a very desolate and lonely place, I thank God you and I are friends. I really need your friendship now, you know, I really do. Yesterday I went down the Slag Club. It wasn't particularly exciting. It's quite an old crowd which is good any rate. If I'd wanted to I could have had this fat girl, but she was a bit too awful really. On the way out she got hold of my neck and tried to drag me into a corner, but I sort of lost interest. And her friends, they were shit, really shit, so I thought, leave it. I didn't even fancy a snog.

I don't have much to say these days. Things seem to wash over me really. The main thing on my mind is the thought of going back up to university for a day, after all this time. I don't really know how I'll cope with it.

I'm slowing down these days as well. I'm sobering up, I'm sleeping more, but I still wake up sweating, desperately lonely and unhappy. I need a nice girl to love me, don't I? That's what I need. Some tall, fit-looking bird with a good dress sense to look after me, to dote on me. But wouldn't we all like that, eh? I was looking up the potential in the Rat's Puke tonight. Not a lot going really. Where's that barmaid who always smiles at me? She looks nice, a bit short and fat maybe, but it looks as though she's got a nice temperament.

Yeah, I've definitely calmed down, I really have.

'What, you come from London? Aah, that place, it's too bloody trendy for me. Smokey, dreary, too much hustle and bustle. It's so bloody unfriendly as well.'

'You Londoners really reckon yourselves, don't you? You cockneys think you're hard bastards, but you won't take us northerners, no way, mon, no way.'

'London, I just don't like it – so unfriendly. It's just too big. I don't like the people, know what I mean?'

'We came down to London, right, looking for a fight, OK, and where were you? We were in Trafalgar Square knocking back the bitter and not one single cockney showed up.'

'Tell you, if you came up our way and opened your mouth with that London accent of yours you'd be fucking dead, mon. Us lot, we're a friendly bunch, mind, but if I were you I wouldn't go in some of the pubs I know with that accent.'

'Of course, like, we're all living in London at the moment. But I tell you, the place is just too full of itself, too busy, too unfriendly. What, you looking for a fight or something? You laughing at my 'tache?'

Ah, London! My home, the place where I was born, where I grew up. London with its superb cultural heritage, embracing all who visit her. How I love you!

This is sad, this is awful. I wanted to tell you about my dog. How brilliant he was, how I grew up with him. But I can't, it just turns into sentimental stuff, you know, it's just no good. I ended up sounding like a children's book, like the ones I always used to read to escape of course. Books whose warm sentiment made me cry. A little boy crying, reading a book. That's what's in me really deep down. But

133

it's no good. It's not impressive, it doesn't say anything about life. It certainly didn't teach me anything about life. And of course I got hurt. But this is really difficult now for me, because that soft sentiment still means so much. It's the sort of thing when you're tucked up in bed on a cold winter's night, and you've got sore red eyes because you've been crying, and you're so desperate to love and be loved.

Anyway, here's another poem, another bloody poem. Maybe you'll see what I mean, it's really sentimental. I wrote it a long time ago. It's a poem that's still inside me, those feelings and all that.

> When cold becomes the year
> Walking
> Outside, seeing breath and listening
> Talking
> Always London's Christmas kindles
> From fingertips to toes warmth mingles
> How warm and hazy and brilliant, sighted
> Peering from the car window, Regent Street lighted
> And now come flushed faces and gleamy eyes
> Strangers all, under the lights that arch the skies
> Unknown they pass, but in common cheer
> When it's cold, things become so clear
> Those once missed become more dear

Well, maybe you see what I mean. But the world just isn't anything like that, dammit. It's how I wanted the world to be, it's that big lovely childhood con again.

But wait a minute, just wait a goddam minute. No no, forget it. For a moment I thought maybe, oh I don't know. It'll be Christmas soon again anyway. If only people weren't so shit, spoiling everything. Their stupid insecurities, fucking everything up.

You know, looking back on those university days, I do remember a few noble things were achieved. If you think about it, a group of young idealists, socialists that our group were, protesting against the corrupt and damaging ways of the government. That's good isn't it? Small groups standing up against a whole horde of institutionalized faceless bullies.

The big thing when I was there was the miners' strike. We all walked around in Coal Not Dole badges. All of us united in the cause. I remember me and Sonny burning a copy of the *Sun* the day the miners were defeated. I know there was a load of bullshit surrounding the whole thing, but it strikes me as being a really noble thing, us supporting the miners. Jesus, I haven't got it together, have I? I can't seem to get across what I mean anymore. Socialism's good and all that, do you see what sort of state I'm in? That's what age and weariness does to you. Socialism is a political and moral principle isn't it? You can't just say it's 'good', can you?

But can you? Because when you start to see individuals clearly, when you start understanding people's characters, things like political concepts become meaningless. They become just sixth-form student stuff, idealism, it just doesn't fit anymore. You just start thinking in terms of 'he's a wanker' and 'she's a piece of shit' and you remember that socialism is a good thing, isn't it? When you see how ludicrous and sick people are, you wonder how anyone could be bothered to think of political concepts. When you see how absurd they are and all that, I mean, it's all a fucking joke, isn't it?

I know what's going on, I'm starting to think what the fucking hell's happened to me? Where did all that learning go? You see, in school they teach you the wrong way round. They teach you about man's great achievements before they teach you about life. So you're learning political theory before you even know what the fuck politics is for and why it was set up in the first place. What! I think I'm starting to . . . I think the drink's . . . all these years of drinking. It's all beginning to wear off. Nah, nah, nah! Of course, firstly, it's true, I have cut down on drinking and therefore I'm beginning to reappraise my thoughts. But secondly, having reappraised them, I remember. Most people are shit, that's what you've got to learn and therefore all concepts, politics and all that stuff, to a large degree it's just meaningless, because the most important factor that's going to affect your life is that most people are shit.

Look, I'm really sorry. All this sudden self-doubt. Maybe I was reflecting your own doubts, perhaps, maybe. Nah! Listen, I'm back together again, seriously.

33

I'm sitting on the station platform not far from Nowhere university and it's raining. It's early evening, I'm going back to London.

I'd wandered around the town. I was trying to think about why it all meant so much to me. It's like Disneyworld, the town. I miss that. It's all true, after all, all those theories of mine about people being awful, shit, stupid, shallow. I keep trying to forget you know. Try not to believe it all. But it's all true.

This is the trip I told you about, you see. I told you I was going back up to university after all these years. Now, I thought as I sat in the union bar eating chicken-flavour crisps, who hasn't betrayed me then? One person, that's all. Only one person hasn't betrayed me and that's probably because he couldn't be bothered or he didn't have the opportunity.

I'm over what I felt then. I mean those terrible, frightening feelings. There's other life about me in London to distract me. Although it doesn't really distract me because I'm always thinking about what went on there.

Some things mean so much to me and nothing to other

people. I stood outside the station just staring, standing still and staring. Now I'm on the train back home to London. It's really good, the train's bombing along with the rain lashing the window. It's quite dark outside already. It's a real laugh. Travelling at night's brilliant, especially when it's raining. Have I told you about this thing I've got about riding in cars? I really love it, it's brilliant. I really love getting driven around in a car, peering out the window, watching the driver, opening the glove compartment, winding down the window, things like that. I really miss that, getting driven about the place.

The university was just sad and bland, and for some moments it was terrifying and sick and a waste. I got this feeling that I wanted to stay up there all night, maybe sleep in a doorway or something. I'd like that, in the same sort of way that I like having some girls. Just a thing to do, prostitute myself, sleep rough. And still the train bombs along and now it's getting pleasantly cold. I love the cold. I love winter, it's easily the best time of year. Summer's for a totally different type of person. I love the winter. Rain, it's brilliant, it's started to stream down the windows and I'm getting all cold, but I'm really warm inside. And Nowhere town and Nowhere university are getting further and further away. And at home I haven't got anything to go back to, no love and no happiness.

So what have you got to look forward to in life? Betrayal, stupidity, vanity, insecurity, that sort of thing? Can males have friends? It doesn't seem like it. Women? I've lost my faith in them. There is one thing that you can get out of life, that will make you walk the streets in triumph, that's what I'm trying to get at. I suppose it's art, creativity, the genius and understanding that comes from suffering. It seems to be man's eternal quest to try and explain this to women, to try and share it and live it with females. Most males are scum of course, and are totally incapable of appreciating or under-standing, but some aren't, and those are the ones you

138

should seek out in life. But the tragedy is that in the main, males don't get on with each other. There's too much rivalry and jealousy and so they turn to women. And do women care?

34

Love, it's really touching. The whole group agree that Pete and Merissa are very definitely in love. Jokes about wedding bells are already being made. They're just never apart, those two. Totally inseparable. They sit with us in our group and smile at each other. It really is touching.

The hot knife sessions continue. Luke wanders round in a permanent dazed state. He even rolls up in the street. Yesterday he told me he hated his stepfather, the day before that he wandered into my room and started opening the cupboards. I asked what he was doing. 'My dope, I'm looking for my dope,' he mumbled and walked out again, out of his head.

Luke's being going out with this girl for a few months now, she sits in on the dope sessions, smiling, always by his side. It's very touching.

I'm starting to hang out with Sonny and his mate, Quentin, a lot. I feel sorry for Quentin, everybody takes the piss out of him, he's a real joke. When we're all stoned we look at him for entertainment, he never touches the stuff but he acts just like a little kid when we're all out of it. I mean, although I've got nothing in common with him and he does behave like a bit of a jerk, I feel sorry for him because of the way the others take the piss. So I'm always extra nice to him, always make sure that I back him up if the others start on him.

One night when everyone had crashed out on dope there was just me and Quentin sitting in the kitchen. I was really pissed and stoned but I was in a generous mood, a friendly, matey mood.

'Quentin mate,' I said cheerily, 'you know you mustn't let them take the piss out of you anymore, you really mustn't. Don't let them get away with it. Seriously.'

I paused and gestured drunkenly in the air, 'you seem to be an all right bloke, really. I think you're OK. I mean,' I leaned forward confidingly, 'quite frankly, Gonza and Triffid, the way they take the piss out of you, don't let it bother you. You see, I think they're a couple of wankers. Gonza's ego is revolting, his ludicrous jealousy and craving for status. And Triffid, well he's just a joke – Gonza's side-kick. Now Sonny's all right, although I wish he wouldn't take this indie music so seriously. I mean, in London no one listens to that stuff anymore, we like soul, which is what these indie merchants despise. But anyway, take my advice, stand up for yourself, don't let them treat you like a joke anymore. God! I'm tired, I'm off to bed, see you tomorrow.'

I stood up to go. Quentin asked me for the 30p I borrowed off him the other day.

'Oh yeah, all right, look, I've probably got it in coppers.'

'No come on Jack, I want it in silver.'

So I went to my room and got him his 30p in silver. Then I went back and crashed out on the bed, totally wasted.

Did I tell you about this special exam paper that I sat last week? I got the result today, an upper second. That means I passed with flying colours! It's really good news because it means I can go on this specialist twentieth-century reading course in London. I really wanted it badly, because the courses here are so boring and the tutors are uninterested. I wrote a formal letter of application for the course to the head of my department today, enclosing my exam result.

The frame of mind I'm in towards academic work here is pretty grim at the moment. This course could mean I might actually get to take it seriously. I mean, I wrote this poem the other day about studying English at degree level. It's quite a short poem and it goes like this:

> The studying of English lit
> Is a load of shit.

Do you know what I mean? Dick Derrick, Dr Patsy Martin, reading a load of crusty old critiques, reading a load of brand-new trendy critiques, it's all a travesty of what literature is all about. It's all the crappy, unimaginative, plagiarized and university brainwashed views of people who generally have no idea about what the writer is talking about. And that's if the writer is any good in the first place! All the shit they make you read, their own personal favourites, all that crap. And when you do get a good writer, and it really inspires you, they just ruin it all by their pathetic run-of-the-mill teaching. What they want is for you to write a standard essay which falls in line with the standard criticisms you have to read through and must also agree with their own standard views and ideas which were themselves given to them by their own tutors and so on and so on. But anyway, at least this new course looks interesting, lucky I got an upper second.

In-depth character description – I don't take it seriously. People are just varying degrees of shit. If someone *is* just shit, then there's no point in analysing them because they'll just have the same boring insecurities that all shit people have. It's what they can achieve that's of interest, how far they can hurt you, what destruction they can cause, that's

142

what you've got to look out for, that's what's important. And then, when you see that, once you know, you can lay down general rules that can protect you. But don't be innocent, don't kid yourself, because the consequences of that can be fatal.

I went into the union building for lunch. On the way I saw Sonny walking across the campus.

'All right, Sonny,' I shouted, 'how goes things?' But for some reason he just walked straight on with a deep frown on his face. I couldn't make it out at all, he *must* have heard me. I went into the refectory, most of the group were sitting at a table near the bar.

'All right everyone,' I said cheerily. Gonza, Triffid, Max, Mick, Jeff and Merissa all looked stonily away in silence. Only Luke and Pete greeted me back. Quentin wasn't there.

I stood quietly watching the group. Triffid started saying something angrily to Gonza, everyone began to talk to each other. Then Pete got up and came over to me. It was incredible, he actually took me aside to talk to me.

'Listen, Jack, I think it's a bit of a bad idea sitting with us anymore. You see Quentin's gone round saying you've been calling us names and saying how much you hate us all. Apparently you've been really slagging off Gonza, Triffid and Sonny.'

'What?' I couldn't believe it. 'Quentin said what? The fucking wanker! What right does he have to bloody go behind my back and grass me up over a few things I said when I was a bit pissed. What the fucking hell, I mean, I never said a word against Sonny and now he just bloody ignored me. It's pathetic. I mean, I don't believe it.'

'Yeah, look Jack, I do know, I really would never say anything to Quentin about other people. Can't you see he's a creep, he's untrustworthy.'

'And I've always been nice to him,' I ranted on. 'I just

143

don't believe it. Everyone else takes the piss out of him except me.'

'I know, I know. Listen, Quentin's gone round saying he's morally obliged to tell people what you've said.'

'He what? I don't believe it, I just don't believe it. That piece of slimy shit. Moral obligation, what a joke. He's only gone round saying this to try and get in with them more.'

'I know, I agree. But at the moment the others don't think so. Sonny's really upset and Gonza's been saying that he can't understand why a good friend like you would want to do a thing like that. At any rate, it's best that you stay well away from them all.'

'I don't believe it, I mean, I just can't believe it. What a joke! What a fucking joke. Where is Quentin anyway?'

'He's gone back home for the week. It's typical of a creep like him, you see. He causes some trouble and then runs away. I'm afraid there's nothing you can do about it, you'll just have to weather the storm.'

Then Pete looked at me suspiciously. 'I mean I don't even know if you were slagging me off. Do you know what I mean? I've got my reservations about Gonza and Triffid but I wouldn't call them wankers. They're all right, you shouldn't start causing friction you know, life's too short. Learn to get along with people, essentially they're nice underneath. You should try and see the good in people.'

I was too stunned to argue. Too shocked and amazed. What a creep Quentin was. How could they take him seriously? What sort of shit goes and does that, it's just fucking incredible. And Sonny! To have Sonny ignoring me, after all the effort I've made to be his friend. Aah. They were all scum, what a fucking joke, Jesus Christ!

'Look, I tell you what,' Pete said, 'we'll go and have a drink and forget it, OK?'

So I went and had a drink with Pete and once again I was amazed by the kindness and decency shown to me. First Luke and now Pete. The only two worthwhile people there.

144

'But why aren't you ignoring me as well?' I asked Pete.

'Because I don't trust Quentin, I'm suspicious of his motives in telling the others what you said.'

So I had a whole load of pints and drunkenly told Pete what a good bloke I thought he was. Then Merissa came over.

'Come on, Pete, what are you sitting with him for, someone who betrays their friends.'

Pete looked embarrassed and went off with Merissa. I understand; girls, they have that power over you, and anyway they were such a devoted couple.

I had some more to drink. I was really pissed by now. I thought, ah sod it, this is stupid. I'll go and apologize. I mean, the whole thing's pathetic. So I went over to their table.

'Look lads,' I said expansively, generously, magnanimously, 'I'm sorry if I said a few things out of order. I was pissed anyway. I hope it's all right.'

'Yeah well, why don't you fuck off!' Triffid shouted. 'Grassing up your friends. If it wasn't for Quentin's honesty and decency we would never know what you thought of us.'

Then Gonza's eyes gleamed and he shouted, 'That's right, you've betrayed your friends. I've got nothing to say to you. Quentin did the right thing in telling us, he . . . '

'Listen, that's a fucking bloody joke. You . . . can't you see . . . I mean, Quentin's obviously a wanker, isn't he? What sort of creep goes round grassing up people behind their backs? I mean, what a fucking joke. It's bloody pathetic. It's so stupid, can't you see?'

'Oh, we're very impressed with you swearing, I'm sure,' said Merissa. 'If you're going to tell us that way why don't you just go somewhere else. I don't think any of us want to speak to someone who betrays their friends.'

'Yeah, that's right, why don't you get lost, Jack.'

The sheer injustice, the fucking unreasonable pathetic

nature of it all. The way they all ganged up, agreed, decided. The way they loved it all, all that mock offence, all that shit. When you're in that sort of position you just can't do a thing.

So I had to go away and from then on I got the full bullshit treatment. Only Luke and Pete would talk to me. I got all these crap, insignificant little turds up in arms against me. People who I'd never spoken to gave me filthy looks because they were friends of Gonza or Triffid, or someone. I tried to talk to Sonny. He just stared at me with fury and walked away. Quentin came back and was the hero of the group. He walked around with a big grin on his face. I mean, Jesus, it's a joke, isn't it? All these weak pathetic people who know nothing, who are just pieces of shit. There's Triffid and Gonza going on about me betraying their friendship. Some friends they were. And Gonza knows it's all bullshit, he knows he was never my friend. But the sly bastard's playing the hurt role all the way along the line.

And Triffid's a stupid thick idiot, and Max, Mick and Jeff are just thick wankers who always hated my intelligence anyway and were dying for an excuse to openly dislike me. And Quentin is just some little insignificant creep who's riding a jammy one. And there's just no reason or justice or sense in it all. Groups are just shit, revolting camps that nurture revolting egos. Group law can stone you to death and ride on a false moral triumph at the same time. Lies can be lived out to the full with the backing of a group. It's just pathetic.

And me, poor bloody me, I was shattered by it all. Stupid isn't it? But I really was shattered. I sat on my own again in the bar, only Luke would say hello, and Pete would come and talk to me for a while. I got to know Pete quite well then. He was a nice sort of bloke although he insisted Gonza and Triffid were OK. He was really in love with Merissa. It was touching.

146

35

Dear Jack

Thank you for your application for the Specialist Twentieth-Century Course to be held in London. Unfortunately I write to tell you that you have not been selected for a place.
Yours sincerely,

Professor B. F. Shithead.

Dear Professor Shithead,

I don't understand at all why I have been rejected for the Specialist Twentieth-Century Course to be held in London, since I got an upper second in the exam which should guarantee me a place on the course.
Yours sincerely,

Jack.

Dear Jack,

In normal circumstances you would, with an upper second grade, be guaranteed a place on the Specialist Twentieth-Century Course to be held in London. However, there has been a special recommendation from a member of staff that you do not sit the course. Therefore I have decided against your inclusion.
Yours sincerely,

Professor B. F. Shithead.

Bastard, bastard, bastard! He's fucking got me. Derrick, that phoney scumbag. I'm going round, I'm going to have it out with him.
I went round.
'Listen, Jack,' Dick said, sitting back in his chair and pouring out a coffee, 'I just don't think you merit a place on the course. Your work shows no enthusiasm for the subject. You're never on time for tutorials, you never say anything, you can't even be bothered to bring in your books. That's why I put in a special recommendation that you shouldn't get on the course. Instead I put down Christobel's name, even though she didn't get a high enough grade. Christobel tries, that's what's important, and that's why she's getting your place.' Dick smiled and sipped his coffee.
I couldn't say anything, I just stood and stared and then I walked out of the room and went down to the off-licence in town. On the way I passed Quentin and Gonza, they were both smiling.

I've only been in to university once this week, and that was a mistake. Seeing all those other poor bloody students traipsing around. The rest of the time I've been spending sitting in my room knocking back vodka, gin and cans of lager. I've stopped going to meals now, it's too awful. I saw

Ian, Adrian and Jonathan the other day. They smiled at me nervously. I couldn't speak to them.

Pete drops round quite a bit to share some of my drink and have a chat. I tell him how pissed off I am about everything and he tells me how nice people really are. In a couple of days Merissa is going to France for a month as part of her course. Pete's been going on about how much he'll miss her.

Hey! Have I told you how awkward it is talking to Pete about all my reservations I've got against him and he's got against me? But the point is that at least he's being a friend and I do really like him.

Anyway Merissa had her big send off today. Her *bon voyage* to France. They were both nearly in tears. I don't know how they're going to cope without each other. There was a whole load of them setting off for France on the platform. One of Pete's mates was going as well.

'Don't worry, Pete, I'll look after her for you,' he said, and gave Pete a matey hug and a kiss on the cheek.

You know I wonder if blandness is a defence mechanism. There are times when a bit of me decides not to understand anymore. To disbelieve, to just drift along, not to question anything, to muddle along and take it all. But you can't stay like that for long, whoever you are, and then you're in for a nasty shock.

So for the next few weeks it was me and Pete. Buddies, pals, chums. We'd sit in each other's rooms. He'd talk about how much he loved Merissa and I'd go on about how awful I thought people were. Every day at lunchtime he'd spend hours waiting by the phone for her to call. We'd sit in his room and get pissed together, we'd toast the health of women, and sing a bit. We'd go into town together and muck about in the shops, we really got on. He liked my humour and intelligence, and I liked his decency and good nature. I told him about the London scene, about music and clubs and clothes, that sort of thing. It was a sort of alliance against loneliness and for decency and friendship.

He'd still hang out with the group, telling me about their gossip and stuff. Sometimes Luke would join us and we'd do hot knives. Most of the time we were pissed or stoned. He told me about Sonny's new girlfriend, about Quentin being taken seriously by the group. Apparently, the big thing now in the group was an anti-Triffid campaign. Started by Quentin and Gonza, the group were always slagging off Triffid.

Today Merissa comes back from France. Pete's in an ecstatic mood. He's been worried for the past week because Merissa hasn't phoned him. I went into town with him before the train was due to arrive. He got all these over the top flowers and cards. The day before he'd been planning what to wear for today. I left him at the gates of the station with all his presents for Merissa.

It's three o'clock in the morning. Pete's sitting in my room, staring into space. We've finished off a bottle of vodka between us.

'I just can't believe it,' he said for the tenth time. 'They got off the train together, he had his arm round her. I mean, that fucking dickhead, that wally, he was supposed to be my friend, he fucking told me he'd look after her for me. I just don't believe it. And she gave me this stupid fucking embarrassed smile. I was standing there with all these flowers and everything. I went round to see her yesterday. She told me she wanted to be just friends. I mean what! Fucking what? Friends! I've only been going out with her for three years. I've only spent the last three years of my life with her! I said what about this bloke, this wanker, how could she hang out with that shit. I said didn't I mean more to her than him.'

Pete paused, his eyes were gazing out of the window, his face was frozen in shock, incredulity. 'She told me, she said, I mean, you're not fucking going to believe this, she said this bloke was special and that he was in love with her and she didn't want to hurt him. I mean, fucking hurt *him*! What about fucking bloody pissing me! I just . . . I can't believe it. Three years, where's all that gone then? I can't believe it. Three fucking years.' Again Pete stopped and froze. 'I asked her if she'd slept with him, she said she had. Do you know what I mean, she sat there and she said she had. I just don't know what to do.'

Pete came round again today. He brought three bottles of wine with him. We sat up till six in the morning. He hadn't eaten or slept for three days.

'I keep ringing her up, her flatmate keeps answering and tells me she doesn't want to speak to me. Christ, Jack, what can I do? I saw her this afternoon with this bloke. I just sat on my own and watched them talking together. I mean, three years, it just doesn't mean anything to her. And this bloke, this cunt, what's he think he's fucking well doing? I just don't know. I keep remembering our holidays together, you know, the times we spent together. It was all so brilliant. I got out all her photos today, us in Holland, that was a brilliant holiday. We spent, I spent the happiest days of my whole life with her and now she won't even talk to me. I keep thinking of her sleeping with that bloke. I can't bear it, Jack. I just can't bear it.'

We went out into town the next night and smashed a load of windows. Pete wouldn't talk much, he'd just stare in front of him all the time.

'Merissa was the only thing that mattered to me, she still is the only thing that matters to me. Why, how does she cheapen herself with these new people? I want to fucking kill that bloke, that cunt. I, you know, it's just terrible. I love her, you see, I really love her. And she, she just doesn't care.'

I'm pissed all the time now, along with Pete. I've stopped going into the campus at all. I wake up about three o'clock and go to the off-licence. I stand in a queue with pensioners and dossers. I'm only a teenager and I'm queueing up with all these oldsters. I can't go on without a drink. I don't even see people anymore. I don't even look at people.

151

'She's loving it Jack, she's fucking loving it. Her friends have all rallied round her. I went up to one of them and she said it was disgraceful the way I kept following Merissa and ringing her up. She said some shit about her being an independent woman and that I should respect that. The fucking indignity of it all. I keep wanting to say That's My Girlfriend. You know, you scum used never to have any say in the matter and now, you're telling *me* what she thinks. You don't even know her. I bloody know her, she's my, she used to be my girlfriend.'

We got stoned really heavily the other night. I don't think Pete's had any sleep for ages now. He hardly eats anything, he looks like death. And me, I've gone really downhill with him. We were stoned and he kept on going on about Holland, his holiday with Merissa there. 'That was the happiest time in my life, you see. I spent it with Merissa, why doesn't she care anymore?'

He started crying, his eyes filled up and he just cried. It was awful.

'She won't even speak to me, she won't even say anything to me. I can't bear it. All I want is for her to speak to me now. I can't understand it. And why does she hang out with that wanker, the two-faced cunt, that slimey treacherous Judas?'

I don't really know what's going on anymore, I just live for my next drink. I wake up and shuffle down to the supermarket to buy my drink. I'm on loads of it. I wander round the town on my own now, even in the evenings. I've got just enough money to go home. I can't stay here any longer. I'll die in this place.

I saw Pete that evening, the evening I was going home to London. He didn't say much. I felt bad about going, leaving him. He said he'd been hanging about with the group. He said he'd go out with them.

I took the train home. Everything was blank around me, the journey home, opening the front door, it all felt like nothing. I couldn't think at all. I just drank all the time.

I was home for a week when I got a phone call from . . . from Merissa. I couldn't believe it.

'Is Pete with you?' she asked coldly. 'Well then, where is he? I've been trying to get some of my things back from his house but nobody knows where he is. It's really tedious and annoying.' She rang off.

And then a week later she called again.

'Hello Jack, er, this is Merissa.' There was a long pause. 'Look Jack, I want you to know that it wasn't my fault, all right? I want you to tell everyone that it wasn't my fault. You must understand that, it's very important.'

'What? What? I don't understand,' but she'd rung off.

I got some money together that day. I tried to find some clean clothes. I got the train back up there. It was like, I don't know, it was like nothing. I walked into the campus. The same stupid crap people, talking, laughing, existing. The first person I saw was Sonny. He tried to look the other way, tried not to catch my eye.

'Where's Pete then?' I asked.

He looked at me surprised, a sort of sickly look.

'I thought you'd know that, since you were supposed to be such good friends with him. He's dead, he's dead in Holland. That's where they found him. Dead in Holland on some drugs overdose or something.' Sonny walked away.

You see, the strange thing was I didn't really believe it at first. You know, when you understand something, when you've got it sussed, but you don't really believe it. So all this phoneyness, all this lies and deceit, they do actually get you and they can kill you. Yes, strange isn't it? They can actually kill you. Gonza and Triffid, and Dick Derrick and Merissa. They can actually kill you. Imagine that, eh! Just imagine that. Well, well, well. What a surprise, eh? These scum, these shit scum can actually kill you.

Now I can't take this. I just can't handle this at all. These fucking scum can actually kill you, you see. Someone actually died. A decent person was actually killed you see. And you know something? I can't handle that, not one bit. I just can't fucking get that at all. You see, OK?

God, I was really drinking now. I'd go into the campus totally pissed and just stare at these people, these hideous creations, these appalling monsters. I'd just go in and sit down and stare. I'd walk around the campus and bloody shout. I'd walk around the town and shout. Oh fucking hell, yes. I didn't sleep, no, I didn't sleep. So they've killed someone eh, they've only killed someone. You fucking turds, you pieces of shit.

I was sitting in this analyst's room, this awful room with a big box of Kleenex placed by my chair. I wonder if you're supposed to cry. I wonder if they want you to cry. This is my third visit here, some woman doctor sits and listens while I try and explain it all.

'You see, for instance, I can look out of the window and see these trees and stuff and they just don't mean anything to me, do you see? I walk across a field and it's just all meaningless. I used to be able to like it, to appreciate it, but now, I just can't you see.'

This woman just sat there with a polite smile on her face. Once, out of the corner of my eye, I'd caught her yawning. I mean, what? Whose sick joke was this? I ended up trying to amuse her for the hour, telling jokes or something. It's pathetic.

Apparently Merissa wept buckets at Pete's funeral. I can really imagine it. She cried on the shoulder of her new boyfriend. Everyone agrees what a devoted couple they are.

I saw her in the union building the other day, sitting with a new group, enjoying all the attention and stature.

'Listen, Jack,' she said to me, 'nobody wants you around here anymore, you know. You've become an embarrassment. Your whole attitude is just selfish and stupid. Why don't you just go away and take your misery somewhere else.'

Then I weakened all of a sudden. I couldn't control it at all. I saw her face and I spat in it and walked out.

'You're a pig, you're an animal, disgusting.'

No one talks to me anymore. They're a very moral lot up here you know. Me, I just wandered around a bit, drinking a lot and then I left. I left university for good and came back here.

So what is delirium then? It's that feeling that day on hot knives, it's dancing to Northern soul. It's the supreme achievement of the mind, it's love. I want to share delirium with a girl, to wake up with her, to be with her all the time. To watch the sun rise and the snow fall and settle.

What am I doing tonight? I'm going out to a club, having a few drinks, chatting up a few girls. I'm better now, by the way, a lot better. I'm over all that terrible anxiety and grief and sadness, I'm getting along. I think what's come out of all this, the most important thing of all, is your friendship. Yes, you and I, that's the best achievement: that I can say . . . you're my friend.